INDIANS OF THE NORTHWEST COAST

INDIANS OF THE

Facts On File
New York • Oxford

NORTHWEST COAST

Photographs by MAXIMILIEN BRUGGMANN
Text by PETER R. GERBER
Translated by Barbara Fritzemeier

1   This figure on a mortuary pole from the Kaigani village of Old Kasaan, Prince of Wales Island, represents the legendary shaman Stone Eagle, who could change himself into other beings. This totem pole now stands in the Totem Heritage Center, Ketchikan.

Cover stamp: "Mythical Thunderbird with Whale." Silk-screen by Susan A. Point, Coast Salish.

Flyleaf: The Haida village of Skidegate, Queen Charlotte Islands. Photograph by George M. Dawson, 1878. (NMM)

Photograph on title page: Evening time south of Prince Rupert on Ridley Island with a view over Chatham Sound.

Abbreviations used in the captions to photographs: See page 232, Acknowledgments.

Concept, Design, Geographic Map: Maximilien Bruggman, Yverdon

Index: Andreas Isler, Zürich

INDIANS OF THE NORTHWEST COAST
First published in the United States in 1989 by Facts On File Publications
Copyright © 1987 by U. Bär Verlag, Zurich (Switzerland) under the title *Indianer der Nordwestküste*
English translation copyright © 1989 Facts On File Publications

Facts On File, Inc.   Facts On File Limited
460 Park Avenue South   or   Collins Street
New York, NY 10016   Oxford OX4 1XJ
USA   United Kingdom

Distributed in Canada by Canadian Manda Group, P.O. Box 920, Station U, Toronto M8Z 5P9

Library of Congress Cataloging-in-Publication Data

Bruggmann, Maximilien.
    [Indianer der Nordwestküste. English]
    Indians of the Northwest coast /
        by Peter R. Gerber ; translated
    by Barbara Fritzemeier ; photography by
        Maximilien Bruggmann.
        p. cm.
    Translation of: Indianer der Nordwestküste / Photos,
        Maximilien Bruggmann ; Text, Peter R. Gerber.
    Bibliography: p.
    Includes index.
    ISBN 0-8160-2028-0
    1. Indians of North America—Northwest Coast of North America.
I. Gerber, Peter R. II. Title
E78.N78B7813 1989
971.1'300497—dc19   89-1330
                                                              CIP

British CIP data available on request.

Facts On File books are available at special discounts when purchased in bulk quantities for businesses, associations, institutions or sales promotion. Please contact the Special Sales Department of our New York office at 212/683-2244 (dial 800/322-8755 except in NY, AK or HI).

Composition by Facts On File, Inc.
Manufactured by Trilogy
Printed in Italy

10 9 8 7 6 5 4 3 2 1

1

WHITEHORSE

YUKON
BRITISH COLUMBIA

N.W.T.

Yakutat Bay

TLINGIT

Skagway
Haines

Glacier Bay

Chichagof Island

Coast Mountains

Stikine River

NORTH

Rocky Mountains

JUNEAU

ALASKA
U.S.A.

Sitka

Baranof Island

Petersburg

Wrangell

TSIMSHIAN

Prince of Wales Island

Hydaburg

Ketchikan
Metlakatla

Nass River

Kispiox
Hazelton
Kitwancool

CANADA

ALBERTA

Dixon Entrance

Port Simpson

HAIDA

Prince Rupert
Masset

Graham Island

Skeena River

PACIFIC OCEAN

Skidegate
Queen Charlotte Islands
Queen Charlotte
Skedans

Hecate Strait

Moresby Island

BELLA COOLA

Anthony Island
Nistints

Bella Coola

Bella Bella

Rivers Inlet

KWAKIUTL

Coast Mountains

Fraser River

BRITISH COLUMBIA

Port Hardy

Alert Bay

| 0 | 100 | 200 | 300 | km |

SCALE

| 0 | 100 | 200 | mi |

Nootka Island

Gold River

NOOTKA

Vancouver Island

Nanaimo

Georgia Strait

Vancouver

Chilliwack

WASHINGTON

MAKAH

Neah Bay

VICTORIA

Seattle

COAST SALISH

U.S.A.

ALASKA

CANADA

U.S.A.

Columbia River

FOREWORD

When the noblemen of Klukwan, the main village of the Chilkat-Tlingit in Alaska, woke up during the night, it is said that they stayed awake into the early morning hours pondering how they could increase their family's wealth and prestige. The chief of an influential house who lacked a daughter would declare the left half of his son's body to be the daughter, in order to be able to pass on titles and privileges which were due only female descendants. Such recollections illustrate that the culture of the Northwest American Natives does not fit within commonly held beliefs about American Indians.

Instead of feathers and horses, this is a world characterized by fish and wood. Riven by fiords and covered with sodden forests, the mountains, which fall steeply into the Pacific Ocean, circumscribe an extraordinary environment. It is only on the Northwest Coast that the native cultures produced professional artists who created works of lasting aesthetic value for the noble families.

Nonetheless, the people of the coast have shared the fate of other native peoples in the New World. Once the first among nations, they have become second-class citizens within wealthy countries whose abundance rests, to a large extent, on the cheap acquisition of land through "discovery." It makes no difference that the once warlike Pacific Coast natives have been degradated through economic dependence rather than through battle.

Today, however, their artists and artisans are being "rediscovered." The pride which is again visible is not only healing some of the wounds of history, but is also opening the way to hope for a better, self-determined future.

2 (Page 6) The famous Kwakiutl chief, Mungo Martin (1881-1962), carved a heraldic totem pole for Thunderbird Park in Victoria that used Tsonoquoa, the woman of the woods, as the base figure. Her face is visible with everted lips to produce her cry, "Oooooh!" The fearsom giantess represents health and wealth at potlatches.

3 Driftwood on the beach of Quadra Island; Rebecca Spit Marine Park, British Columbia.

Dr. Christian F. Feest, Museum für Völkerkunde, Vienna.

9

INTRODUCTION

A sunbeam penetrates the rain-heavy clouds which darken the sky; tendrils of fog drift along the steep mountain sides. The scenery changes from a gloomy gray to a shimmering glow. It spreads across an ocean that glitters and reflects the light as though Raven Yel, the divine trickster of the Northwest Coast Indians, had scattered a million crystals to amuse himself and the human beings. But the illusion passes quickly as rain squalls strike our faces, and the wind whips up from the nearby fiord. A cruise boat appears like a ghost between two rocky islands, making for the safe harbor. The present crowds out memories of the mythical past. For centuries, this natural drama of the eternal and impressive Pacific Northwest Coast has repeated itself; it seems untamable by human hands. This constancy is also reflected in the unique culture of the people who have lived on this coast for centuries and have adapted themselves to it.

Adaptation and continuity, tradition and change, these are the hallmarks of the history and culture of the Tlingit, Tsimshian, Haida, Kwakiutl, Nootka and Coast Salish, to whom the text and photographs in this book are dedicated. Together these groups of people form the culture area of the Northwest Coast Indians, taking in a territory from Yakutat Bay to the Olympic Peninsula, from the 60th to the 46th latitude, overall a distance of about 2,000 km (1,200 miles). South of this area lived (and, in part, continue to live), tribes who share some aspects of this culture, but who were also strongly influenced by two other neighboring cultures, the Plateau and California Indians. For this reason they have not been included here.

Although "discovered" by Europeans only 246 years ago and not thoroughly studied until 100 years ago, the people of the Northwest Coast, especially the Kwakiutl, are among the most documented Indian cultures of North America, about whom a rather uniform image has been transmitted over time. This image has come to be seriously questioned in the last three decades. Much that seemed to be certain and explained is now open to doubt and is often found to have been based on dubious perceptions. Since this scientific process is ongoing, this book can only indicate areas of uncertainty in ethnographic knowledge about Northwest Coast Indians; it cannot resolve them. Unfortunately, many questions must be left unanswered. We do, however, want to bear witness to the fascinating way of life that these peoples have developed and have carried into the present, despite the intense shocks they have suffered from contact with the "white man." For those of us who stand on the outside looking in, this is most clearly illustrated in the art of these people, which has no equal on the entire continent, excepting perhaps the ceramic work of the Pueblos.

The continuity of the Northwest Coast cultures is not only apparent in their bizarre and foreign-seeming wood carvings—masks, rattles, chests, canoes, totem poles, and other art work, but also in a growing self-awareness in the descendants of humbled generations, whose land and resources have been contested since the first contact. Indian people still suffer from the cultural uprooting and social disruption brought on by the decimation of their people through European diseases such as measles, smallpox and influenza, as well as through the degradation occasioned by the political effects of colonialism. Now they are demanding recognition of their right to be Indian, to be allowed to live in self-determined autonomy, on their own land, and with the guaranty that they be allowed to develop their own resources, particularly fish and wood. These legitimate demands lead the observer beyond a purely folklorish admiration of their artistic creations. In the United States and Canada, Indian people are developing into a politically powerful group whose demands have international implications, raising issues of international law as to their status as indigenous peoples.

We therefore feel ourselves strengthened in our purpose of dealing with this fight for survival in a colonial setting, as well as in the present time, and in providing a historical view of the life styles of the original inhabitants of the Northwest Coast. We will document the transition from a strict hierarchical social order to an egalitarian form of communal existence; the changes in their most important economic activity, fishing; as well as the continuity in traditional forms of artistic expressions. In their will to survive, the Northwest Coast peoples have proven that, after years of cultural destruction in a ruthless "white world," they have not lost the courage to maintain their identity as Indians.

4 With backlighting late in the afternoon, the island-studded coast is transformed into a fairy tale landscape. The photograph was taken on Sitka Sound in southeast Alaska.

5 The mild, rainy climate favors the growth of thick vegetation such as the ferns, moss and lichen in this intensely green forest in Olympic National Park in the state of Washington.

6 Along the Pacific coast the bald eagle rules the air. The wing span of a female is more than 4 meters (13 feet), but in spite of its 7,000 feathers it barely weighs 6 kilograms (13 pounds). The bald eagle can sight its prey at a distance of 800 meters (2,700 feet) and, on descent, can reach a speed of 160 kilometers (95 miles) an hour. Fascination with the bald eagle helped to make it the symbol and heraldic animal for Northwest Coast Indians as well as the symbol of the United States. The photograph was taken on Skowkona Mountain, northwest of Queen Charlotte City.

7 Another powerful heraldic animal is the bear, the largest land animal on the coast. Two species are common: the grizzly bear (*Ursus arctos*) and the slightly smaller black bear (*Ursus americanus*). Both species like fishing for salmon. The protein-rich salmon is instrumental in allowing the bears to reach their extraordinary size. The bear pictured is a specimen of the largest type of black bear found in America. It is found only on the Queen Charlotte Islands and prefers swampy forests.

8 Morning at Sedgwick Bay experienced during a helicopter ride to the most important cultural monument of the Haida, the ruins of Ninstints on Anthony Island, at the southern tip of the Queen Charlotte Islands.

9 Up to the turn of the century, Ninstints was the main village of the Kunghit-Haida. Only a few decaying totem poles bear witness to the past importance of the community. It is still possible to see the hollows at the top of these five mortuary poles where the deceased person was placed behind a vertical plank (see photo 55). Thanks to old photographs, the figures on the poles are identifiable. On the first pole (moving from left to right) the wings of an eagle are visible, although the head has lost its beak. The fearsome jaws of a killer whale can be discerned on the second pole, and the third and fifth poles each has a bear carved on it.

10 These corner posts and roof beams of one of the 20 houses once standing in Ninstints have been reclaimed by nature.

11 On this detail of a fallen totem pole in Ninstints, a frog peers playfully from under the mighty tail fin of a killer whale. Forty years ago the delicately carved details on the frog's head—the large eyes and small nostrils—were still clearly visible.

12 Depicted on another mortuary pole in Ninstints is a bear protecting a small child and lovingly licking the child's head.

13 It is only possible to guess what the heraldic animal on this badly weathered totem pole at the edge of the forest might be. The two upper incisors tell us that it must be a beaver. A frog sits between his front legs. Barely recognizable between its hind legs with their clawed feet are the flat tail with typical cross-hatching and a face.

▷ The idea that the first humans lived in a shell is a frequently recurring theme in the various creation myths of the Northwest Coast Indians. This small bone figure, 41 mm (2 inches) high, was dug up together with its protecting shell at Ozette, the archaeological site on the Olympic Peninsula. It is on exhibit at the Makah Museum (see pages 33-35).

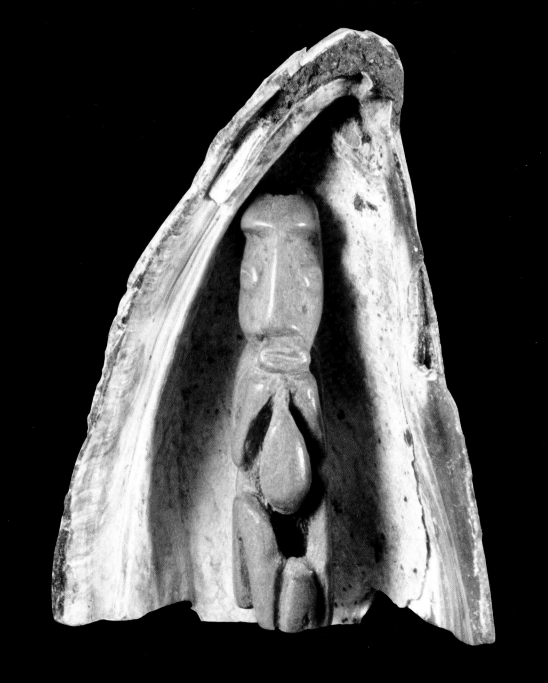

5

6 △

7 ▽

Raven Yel was walking along the beach one day. He was bored, and in his irritation he called to heaven, which, to his surprise, answered him, although it was only a muffled croak. Curious, he looked around and saw a giant shell at his feet. It opened a crack and he saw that it was full of tiny beings who were peering out fearfully. Yel was happy for the diversion and began to coax with the gentle tongue of the schemer, enticing and urging the inhabitants of the shell to come out and play with him. It was not long before first one being and then others, shyly and very fearfully, ventured out of the shell. They were strange creatures: two-legged like Raven Yel, but without his shining feathers. Covered only with pale skin, they were naked except for the long black hair on their round, beak-less heads. Instead of wings they had stick-like appendages. But Yel was satisfied and very happy with his new playmates—the first people.

ANCESTORS

A ferry trip along the coast reveals a landscape that is simultaneously attractive and confusing. Hundreds of islands, countless bays, narrow inlets between steep mountain slopes, dangerous ocean tides, shoals, storms and impenetrable fog require that the navigator have a good geographic memory and even a special sixth sense, not to mention luck. The dark coniferous forests which cover the steep banks appear gloomy and inhospitable, often hiding signs of human habitation: the fishing villages and lonely cabins. The sometimes narrow, sometimes wide river valleys provide views of the snow-covered coastal range. Torrential rivers plunge over rocks and force themselves through narrow gorges in their race to the sea. In the north, glaciers calve directly into the coastal waters. The Stikine, Nass, Skeena, Fraser and Columbia, the five mightiest rivers, open the way inland where, protected from the rough and stormy west winds that batter the coastal ranges, the climate is more inviting than that of the few narrow beaches and low islands on the coast that are inhabited.

However wild the country appears, the climate is relatively mild. The Kuroshio, a warm ocean current that originates in Japan and sweeps along the west coast, warms the shoreline as far north as the Aleutian Islands in Alaska. The damp ocean air released by the current rises up the coastal mountains, cools off and unloads its wet cargo over the length of the coast. The average rainfall is above 655 cm (260 inches). This oceanic rainy climate is comparable to that of the Atlantic coast of Norway, where the Gulf Stream is responsible for the mild, rainy climate. In the summer the average temperature does not rise above 18°C (64°F) and damp fog often penetrates all clothing. Longer periods of dry weather are rare. The winter temperature of about 0°C (32°F) is easily bearable, but it rains steadily, as though the unpredictable Raven Yel intended to repeat annually the great flood that he loosed over the first humans, as told in the origin myth of the Tlingit.

The coastal waters are teeming with fish, sea mammals and water birds. The rivers, too, pulsate with life. The most impressive occurrence is the annual return of the Pacific salmon, the main sustenance

The Haida myth retold on the opposite page finds its most beautiful visual expression in this 2m- (6.6 feet) high sculpture in white cedar created by artist Bill Reid for the Museum of Anthropology in Vancouver. Dedication festivities for this masterpiece were held in 1980.

of the coastal Indians. The salmon migrate up the rivers in large numbers to their spawning grounds. They are so plentiful that a European pioneer reported being able to cross the rivers on their backs.

The rugged coast, studded with islands, has its geological origin in the continuation of the Continental Divide between the North Pacific plate and the North American continental plate, a tectonic rift that achieved notoriety with the 1980 eruption of Mount St. Helens in the state of Washington. The area, prone to both earth and sea quakes, is dominated in its full length by two mountain ranges. The Mesozoic coastal range forms one of these ranges, which also includes long, narrow, mountainous Vancouver Island. During the winters, this mountain range protects the coast from the cold continental climate, but it also operates as a virtually insurmountable barrier to inland areas. In British Columbia this mountain range does not exceed 4,000 meters (13,200 feet), but in Washington it soars up again in the Cascade Mountains and the marvelous volcanic peaks, reaching a height of 4,392 meters (14,410 feet) with Mr. Rainier.

The second mountain range does not reach as far as the continental coast. It has its beginning in the St. Elias Mountains, of which Mt. Logan, at 6,050 meters (19,850 feet) is Canada's highest mountain. The mountain range continues in the magnificent glacier country of Glacier Bay. South, the range is visible in the many mountainous islands of the Alexander Archipelago and, even farther south, the Queen Charlotte Islands that loom out of the ocean. Then it apparently sinks out of sight completely. The same tertiary plate, however, rises out of the Pacific waters again in the form of the Olympic Range on the Olympic Peninsula in the northwest corner of Washington.

A mountainous, rugged, coastal landscape splintered into numerous islands, with a rainy, mild oceanic climate and plentiful flora and fauna, has been the home of Northwest Coast Indians for centuries. In this environment they have developed cultural characteristics that are not found anywhere else on the North American continent.

The People

When European explorers reached the Pacific coast, they not only had the stormy and obscure coast to contend with, but they also had to deal with the natives, who proved to be extremely confident, aggressive and extraordinarily adept at trade. The inhabitants of this coast were not a unified people and did not represent a single nation. They were, rather, village communities of varying size and structure, which at times would enter into loose confederations with neighboring villages, and at other times carried on wars against them. The literature often refers to "tribe," a term that, in the Northwest, is best replaced with the concept "clan." In the following table, "people" or "nation" designates a region in which the various communities speak languages belonging to the same language family or branch of such a

Viewed from an airplane, this is the eastern section of the glaciers at Glacier Bay National Park in southeast Alaska.

27

People/ Nation	Subgroups (including "Tribes")	Phylum (groupings of similar language families)	Language Family (Language branch)	Language or Dialect
Tlingit	Yakutat, Chilkat, Sitka, Stikine and 10 other "Tribes"	Na-Dene or Tlingit	Tlingit-Isolat	local dialects
Tsimshian	Niska, Gitksan, Coast Tsimshian, Southern Tsimshian	Penutian or Tsimshian	Tsimshian-Isolat	River-Tsimshian Coast Tsimshian Klemtu
Haida	Kaigani True Haida Kunghit	Na-dene or Haida	Haida-Isolat	Kaigani Masset Skidegate
Bella Coola	Bella Coola Tal-io Kimsquit	Unknown	Salish	Bella Coola
Kwakiutl	Haisla Heiltsuk southern or true Kwakiutl	Unknown	Wakashan (Kwakiutlan)	Haisla Bella Bella Kwakiutl
Nootka	Nootka Nitinat Makah and 17 other "groups"	Unknown	Wakashan (Nootkan)	Nootka Nitinat Makah
Coast Salish	Comox, Sechelt Pentlatch, Squamish, Halkomelem, Nooksack, Straits Salish, Puget Sound Salish	Unknown	Salish (Coast Salish)	14 different languages

language family. "Tribe" refers to the different social groups, ranging from a single village to confederations of several such communities, or to an established regional designation.

On the ethnographic map, "people" or "nations" are defined by means of clearly defined regions within which the various communities speak languages or dialects belonging to the same language family. When historical data about the political structure of an area is not available, an ethnographic grouping based on linguistic criteria is often the only possible means of definition. The table, therefore, shows ties based only on language; it gives no information about the political relationships between groups. By comparing individual languages, linguists are able to find similarities between language structures, which, in turn, define a basic language, called "phylum" by linguists. Within a phylum, similarities between languages can generally be further categorized into more narrow groupings called language "families." The linguistic similarities within a language family are, however, purely academic; in reality, speakers of different languages within a single family can rarely understand one another.

These language regions are, therefore, not social or political territories, particularly since at the time of contact, the coastal natives had no national or territorial consciousness. The village communities were completely able, however, to determine and defend their specific environment, which extended mainly to their fishing places, hunting territory and areas where plants valuable to the community could be found.

It is only in more recent times that the concept of "nation" can be substituted for "people" since, for instance, all of the people speaking the Tlingit language are becoming aware of their common traditions. Together they are exhibiting a growing self-awareness as they fight for recognition of their legitimate demands to their ancestral territory and the natural resources available therein. The communities of Native Americans in Canada, for 100 years degraded to "bands," the term used in Canada's Indian Act, have in recent years given voice to a newly developed sense of identity and have thrown up a challenge by referring to themselves as the "First Nations." With this they are emphasizing the long history of their existence on American soil, which lends considerable legitimacy to their demands for the right to self-determination within the Canadian confederacy.

29

The Ancestors

In Indian myths the creator deposits his creatures on the coast, which has been the home of human beings since the beginning of time. "We have always been here," the contemporary descendants say. Archaeological finds substantiate a human presence over several thousand years, but also suggest the possibility of migrations to the coast from the plateau region or the Columbia River Valley in what is now the state of Washington. Nomadic groups of hunters were the first to reach the Northwest Coast. Over a period of time they changed into fishing societies, although it is not entirely clear when this transition took place. Three decades ago, researchers were convinced that the Northwest Coast was inhabited not earlier than 2,500 years ago. Older archaeological sites had not been found or were restricted to the southern coastal region, and the northwest culture area continued to be one of the little researched areas of North American archaeology. Since then several spectacular archaeological finds in the northwest corner of Washington and in southeast Alaska have radically changed these perceptions, proving that human habitation existed 1,000 to 12,000 years ago.

In order to better explain the prehistory of the Northwest Coast,

Bowl made of soapstone dating from the pre-Columbian period of 400-1200 A.D., found in the Fraser Valley near Aldergrove; presumed to have been the property of a Coast Salish shaman. (Lent by J. Yoshioka; 19 cm; MOA)

one must consider it as part of the prehistory of the entire continent. It is generally accepted that prior to Christopher Columbus, America was "discovered" and settled several times. However, there is uncertainty as to when these discoveries occurred. The generally accepted theory is that the first immigrants came from northeast Asia during the last ice age. Known as the Wisconsin Ice Age, this period of glaciation covered the northern half of the continent, with the exception of Alaska, with an enormous sheet of ice. During this time, warmer periods alternated with colder ones, a fact which supports the theories that people could actually reach the continent, and that their cultures could thrive and grow. The first supposition is dependent on a cold period, during which the enormous ice masses caused a general drop in the water level of the ocean by more than 1000 meters (330 feet), creating a land bridge, called Beringia. Two to four such cold periods occurred, which allowed nomadic hunters to enter the continent through Beringia. It may be assumed that the first humans to migrate to America did so accidentally by following the wild animal herds searching for food in the tundras. Once on the new continent, these people soon faced an insurmountable barrier of ice. The second assumption is that during the warmer period, the ice separated into the northeast Laurentian Glacier and the western Cordilleran Glacier, creating an ice-free corridor to the south through which people and animals could move to warmer regions.

When did the first human immigration to America occur? Did Homo erectus, who survived arctic conditions as early as 200,000 years ago, first reach this continent, or was it Homo sapiens, meaning the Neanderthal, who likewise survived an arctic climate 100,000 years ago? Several controversial finds, dating back more than 70,000 years, at least permit speculation that humans of either species could have migrated to America. There is no certain data to support this theory, but other "impossible" archaeological theories have been substantiated over time. It is generally accepted today that humans resembling modern man, Homo sapiens, were present in America more than 30,000 years ago.

A further development in archaeological research plays an important role in the history of the settlement of the Northwest Coast. There is increasing dissatisfaction with the theory that the first Americans could only have reached the continent by the overland route on foot. Research into the history of Australia has brought about the surprising knowledge that the first Australians arrived from southeast Asia by boat more than 40,000 years ago. It is presumed that, in addition to the land route, the first Americans also used the sea route, following the coast. This is reasonable insofar as the coast was probably largely free of ice and less rugged than it is today. It can, therefore, be assumed that in the course of several centuries, immigrants arrived in waves—on foot and by boat. One of these groups, a late arriving, larger population wave of Na-dene (Athapaskan) speaking people, reached the Canadian tundra and forests about 8,000 years ago. Several groups of these Athapaskans migrated south to the Amer-

Innumerable petroglyphs have been found on the Northwest Coast. Only in the rarest of cases is it possible to determine their age. Two killer whales are recognizable in the upper photograph, and the figure to the right probably represents a pregnant gray whale. These petroglyphs were found near the deserted Makah village of Ozette.

In Petroglyph Park in Nanaimo, located on Vancouver Island, the figures shown in the lower photograph are particularly interesting. The largest of them may represent Wasco, a creature which is part wolf and part killer whale.

31

ican southwest and are considered to be the ancestors of the Navajo.

North America has, then, been inhabited for at least 30,000 years, and the Northwest Coast has seen human habitation for 12,000 to 15,000 years. Settlements on the coast developed from south to north, as plateau hunters followed the Columbia River to the coast and, becoming a fishing society, gradually extended their territory northward. As the archaeological site at The Dalles on the lower stretch of the Columbia River and the remains of a mastadon hunt found on the north side of the Olympic Peninsula indicate, this process must have occurred 10,000 to 12,000 years ago. New sites discovered farther north|are more recent in age.

Surprisingly, on a site at Ground Hog Bay in southeast Alaska, the artifacts were more than 10,000 years old. This find, taken together with the linguistic structure of Northwest Coast native languages, gives rise to speculation of a second migration pattern, from north to south. This push to the south may have been made by a part of the immigration that occurred at the end of the glaciation period. The controversial group of the Tlingit and Haida languages in the Na-dene language phylum permits speculation that a relationship exists between these coastal peoples and the later immigrating Athapaskans, who also speak a Na-dene language. Coastal people whose linguistic origins cannot be determined, such as the Wakashan and Salishan, may have arrived at their later-established territories by traveling south. On the other hand, the Tsimshian, who speak a Penutian language, are probably the descendants of people who made their way up the coast from the south, since most Penutian-speaking people live on the American West Coast and are clearly part of an older generation of immigrants dating from the ice age.

The prehistory of the Northwest Coast is divided into three phases. The first phase lasted from the beginning, approximately 12,000 years ago, to about 5,000 years ago, a time when the post glacial climate was gradually stabilizing and the sea level was approaching its current level. Only a few known archaeological sites date from this period, but they show that the Queen Charlotte Islands, located 80 km (48 miles) from the continental coast, and the islands of the Alexander Archipaelago were inhabited as long ago as 9,000 and 10,000 years respectively. Although the sites contained few artifacts, the rough stone work found on the southern part of the coast indicates that these people originated inland and came from the south. By contrast, sites on the northern part of the coast contain micro-blades, small razor-sharp tools worked from obsidian and flint. The micro-point tradition originated in the Old World and is found in Alaska, which supports the idea that these coastal people originated in the north.

In the middle period, from 5,000 to 1,500 years ago, the coastal people gradually developed all of the unique cultural characteristics typical of these areas: an economy specializing largely in fishing and utilizing advanced food preservation methods; a society stratified into classes; the utilization of wood as the most important raw material; and an extensive trade network along the coast and into the interior. As of about 3,500 years ago, it is particularly true that southern coast peoples, settling between Puget South and the Georgia Strait, developed successive cultural traditions. The more recent the origin of the discovered artifacts, the more they resemble those items from the historical period that are preserved in museums. In the most recent sites, an increasingly large number of artifacts were found made of organic material such as wood, bone, horn and bark fiber. Covered with water or mud, they were preserved from decay. Most of the stone sculptures also stem from this period, which has led some archaeologists (taking other factors into consideration as well) conclude that the high point of cultural development on the Northwest Coast occurred during the Locarno Beach phase (3,500 to 2,500 years ago) and the Marpole phase (2,500 to 1,500 years ago). In the course of the last period of 1,500 years, cultural diversity has lessened. Whether changing from stone to wood sculpture is considered a step backwards is subject to doubt.

Ozette—An Archaeological Treasure

One of the most revealing discoveries is the Makah village of Ozette, located south of Cape Flattery on the Olympic Peninsula, deserted since 1920. This village might have been the oldest permanently-inhabited Indian village in North America if its inhabitants had not been forced to relocate to the nearby village of Neah Bay (because the government decided to build a school there). A catastrophe that occurred in Ozette 500 years ago has become today a truly extraordinary windfall for archaeologists. At that time a mud slide, possibly resulting from an earthquake, buried several houses, creating a kind of North American Pompeii. In an exemplary cooperative effort, Washington University in Pullman, which is responsible for the scientific excavation, and the Makah community of Neah Bay worked together to recover and preserve 65,000 artifacts, from house planks to ceremonial items.

The Makah and their ancestors, like other Nootkan-speaking communities, had specialized in whaling. Makah elders are providing valuable help with identifying objects they and their parents and grandparents once made using traditional implements. The scientists decided not to allow the excavated artifacts to disappear into some museum or research institute, but to give them back to the Makah, the only legitimate heirs, for safekeeping. For this purpose, a special museum was planned together with the Makah. In 1979 the new Makah Cultural and Research Center opened with great ceremony. Here the material preserved at Ozette continues to be studied and exhibited along with other artifacts.

All five of these artifacts were excavated at Ozette. They provide us with a glimpse of Makah culture. From top to bottom, the first item is a wooden bowl for fish oil (31 cm [12 inches]), below which is a club carved of yew with three owl faces, which was probably used for ceremonial purposes (44 cm [18 inches]). To the right is a gouging tool that utilizes a beaver tooth for the blade (18 cm [7 inches]); a comb made of a deer antler (13 cm [5 inches]); and a double-sided comb made of whalebone (14 cm [6 inches]).

Page 34: An Ozette longhouse has been reconstructed inside of the Makah Cultural and Research Center. The wall and ceiling planks were movable and could be shifted to suit the weather conditions. Fish were hung from the ceiling rafters for drying or smoking. Living areas and fire pits were separated from each other so that several families could occupy the same house.

Pages 36-37: This silk-screen by the Tsimshian artist Roy Vickers, shows a Chinook salmon with eggs before spawning.

The fisherman in his canoe, a fish spear in his hand, sees the salmon jump and speaks to him:

"Haya, Haya! Come up again, Swimmer, that I may say 'Haya' according to your wish, for you wish me to say so when you jump, Swimmer, as you speaking kindly to me when you jump, Swimmer."

The salmon hears the prayer and jumps again. "Haya, Haya!" And the spear flashes across the water.

SALMON AND CEDAR

Pre-industrial societies are formed by and dependent on the natural environment to a much greater degree than can be imagined. This observation, without a doubt, applies to the cultures of the Northwest Coast. Although the mild, rainy Pacific climate creates a fruitful land and water environment where plants and animals thrive, it is not a Garden of Eden, despite the impression given in many books by recognized American anthropologists. They often stated that the Northwest Coast Indians had an arduous time only during approximately four summer months, when they worked from early morning until late evening to catch the salmon. These fish swam through the rivers in such numbers that it was necessary only to "harvest" them. According to these anthropologists, the rest of the year was spent in leisure and in celebrating the many feasts.

This erroneous portrait has been revised in recent years. For most of the coastal peoples, such rosy conditions never existed. The natural abundance did not produce an egalitarian social order, but a hierarchy, which awarded possessions and luxury to the noble families, while the commoners and slaves lived a miserable existence. American anthropologists avoided the questions of social structure with inadequte descriptions and analyses of the conditions on the Northwest Coast prior to contact with non-Indians, although the lack of data available from that period excuses a great deal. Today Indians are themselves questioning earlier descriptions of their society and culture and are, without illusions, describing their original inequitable social system. Indian authors of a book about traditional food sources and preparation and preservation techniques, for example, spoke openly about their earlier class system.

What are the sources for these contradictory representations of Northwest Coast cultures? As was mentioned earlier, the environment with its plentiful ocean life is responsible for the characteristic economic and social systems. The warm Kuroshio current creates ideal conditions for the varied marine life. Innumerable sea mammals—gray, finback, humpback, and killer whales, porpoise, dolphins, walrus, sea lions, seals and sea otter—populated the coastal waters. Ocean fish, such as cod, halibut, flounder, smelt, sturgeon, herring and eulachon, were equally plentiful. Finally, like a biblical

Jumping salmon with a human face illustrates the Indian belief that salmon, like all animals, are humans in other forms; detail of a silk-screen by Susan A. Point, Coast Salish.

miracle, enormous numbers of the Pacific salmon swim toward the mouths of the rivers annually in order to spawn in the sweet water rivers and, in contrast to other species of salmon, to die there. With few exceptions, each salmon will seek out the river which it swam down three to four years earlier on its way to the ocean. The salmon's sense of direction remains a scientific mystery in spite of the existing theory that the varying organic compositions of the water of various rivers serve as an orientation guide.

Salmon was and continues to be, by far, the most important source of nourishment of the Indian of the North Pacific Coast, although the percentage of salmon consumed, as opposed to other foods, varies from people to people. The Haida of the Queen Charlotte Islands, for example, rely more on ocean fish, such as halibut, while the Gitksan Tsumshian, as river dwellers, are highly dependent on the salmon. There is no question, however, that the life cycle of the salmon was greatly respected along the entire coast, a fact richly reflected in mythology and ceremonies. The mythological and religious relationship between man and salmon is not only expressed in the salmon prayer found at the beginning of this chapter, but achieves meaning in the careful following of prescribed behavior, i.e., throwing of the fish skeleton back into the ocean or river. All of the north Pacific coast peoples believed that the salmon were actually people with eternal life who lived in a large house far under the Pacific Ocean. In spring they put on their salmon disguise and offered themselves to humans as food. The tribes believe that when entire fish skeletons are returned to the water, they will wash back into the sea and the salmon sprits will again change into salmon people in the great ocean house. In this way, the cycle can begin again the following year.

There are five different species of Pacific salmon. These are the great Chinook or spring salmon (*Onocorhynchus tshawytscha*, weighing more than 8 kilograms [18 pounds]), the chum salmon (*O. keta*, weighing more than 5 kilograms [11 pounds]), the coho or silver salmon (*O. kisutch*, weighing more than 4 kilograms [9 pounds]), the sockeye or red salmon (*O. nerka*, weighing about 3 kilograms [7 pounds]), and the pink or humpback salmon (*O. gorbuscha*, about 2.5 kilograms [6 pounds]). The behavior of these salmon varieties has been closely studied by marine biologists in recent years. The studies show that these five types of salmon are not equally plentiful everywhere on the coast. Becasue of its size, the Chinook salmon, for example, avoids the small island rivers of the Alexander Archipelago. There are also annual fluctuations in the number of fish, and their arrival on the coast is unpredictable. The sockeye salmon is the most dependable, arriving in the middle of summer and continuing their migration into fall, allowing Indian fishermen to enjoy a several-months-long harvest. The coho and pink salmon are less reliable. During a brief 10- to 14-day period each year, they appear along the coast and in the rivers. The time of their appearance is unpredictable, but they arrive in large numbers.

Artist Susan A. Point's work has been strongly influenced by traditionally carved spindle whorls. Here are four salmon jumping around the spindle hole. Silk-screen, 1981.

Based on these studies, it is assumed that the famines talked about in myths and in the oral tradition are likely to be factual. This detracts somewhat from the theory of paradisal surplus. In addition to these ecological shifts in the availability of food, the occurrence of forest fires and attacks by aggressive neighboring communities, and exceptionally long, cold winters could lead to a food shortage. The Gitksan maintain that there are no families among their ancestors who do not boast of a hero who saved the family or the entire village from starvation by finding the much-hoped-for food source. One function of the potlatch may have its source here as well. The potlatch is a special form of gift giving, and several instances are documented where a community with surplus food provided a starving village with badly needed food by means of a potlatch ceremony.

On their way to the spawning streams, the salmon jump the falls at Kettle Falls. The Colville Indians fish here with traps and spears. As Inland Salish, they have much in common with the Coast Salish. Oil painting is by Canadian artist Paul Kane, 1810-1871. (1841; ROM)

Page 42: In the Indian River near Sitka, a fisheries expert fishes for marked humpback salmon as part of the research into the mysterious life cycle of the salmon.

Page 43: ". . . one/you can cross the river on their backs . . ."

The natural plenty that the north Pacific coast usually provided was merely the basis for adequate nourishment. At least as important as availability of food were the methods of catching and preserving fish and wildlife. Compared to other hunting and fishing cultures, the Indians of the Northwest Coast, along with the Inuit, developed the most advanced technology for securing and preserving foods. After all, they have been fishing for salmon for 8,000 years, have made intensive use of fish for 4,000 years, and have used preservation methods for at least 2,000 years.

Fishing Techniques

The sheer variety in fishing methods could fill many volumes and simultaneously demonstrates cultural differences between coastal people. It also illustrates, once again, that generalization, despite the

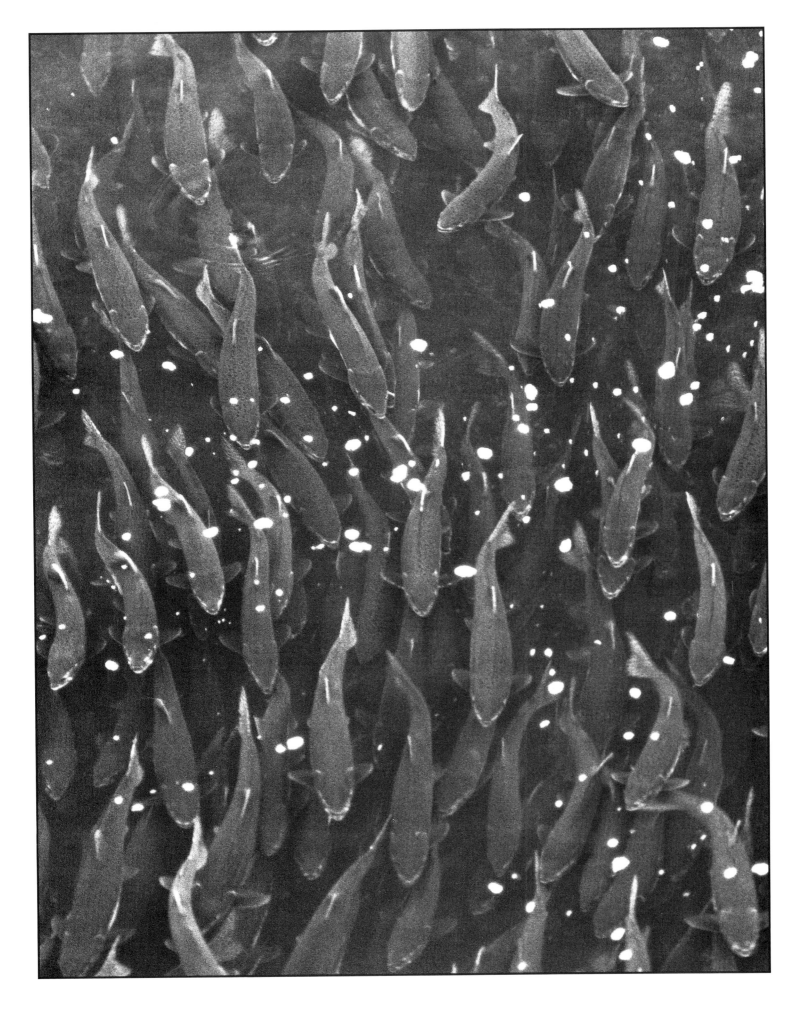

cultural similarities between people in this area, is inappropriate. The variations in techniques and fishing implements is predicated first on ecological conditions, on the local characteristics of the coast or the river banks: their width, depth and the swiftness of the current, to mention just a few factors. Various types of fishhooks, spears, harpoons, nets and traps were used everywhere.

Early hooks were fashioned from the forks in branches or from two pieces of wood. A third type was made by steaming the wood and then bending it. Specialized hooks were used for different types of fish that were caught by means of a rod and hook. Of special anthropological interest are the unusual halibut hooks used by the northern coastal people and the wooden clubs which were used to kill halibut, as well as sea lions and seals. These hooks and clubs were often elaborately carved so that they are as much art objects as tools.

Fish traps and weirs were the most effective means of catching the thickly migrating salmon. The fish, as they swam upriver toward their spawning streams, were forced into the traps through one or several narrow openings (the number of openings depended on the width of the river). Once trapped, the fish could move neither forward nor backwards and were easily caught with a net or spear. A similar system was devised for a narrow bay. During ebb tide, a stone weir or a fence would be constructed. During the flood tide, the weir or fence would be well covered with water, so that the fish could swim over it. But when the tide ebbed, the fence or weir blocked the route to the sea and the fish were trapped.

In addition to the simple dip net, used as a working tool for one person, the Indians used as well other types of nets. For example, a variant of the net sack was used, in which the mesh of the net is elongated and becomes an increasingly narrow tube until finally, there is insuffficient room for the fish to turn around. These long tubular nets were usually fastened onto stakes and were only lifted out of the water when the net was full of fish.

Herring and eulachon (also known as candlefish since, if supplied with a wick, this fish is so oily that it will, in fact, serve as a candle) travel in schools and are caught with gill nets. The spaces in the webbing are large enough so that a fish can swim into the net but not through it. The fish gets stuck going forward and, because its gills work like a barbed hook, it cannot back out either. These nets, measuring several yards in length, are stretched across a river and fastened on the shore. Even in a strong current, they remain perpendicular, thanks to wooden floats and heavy stone sinkers.

Harpoons are used for large fish and sea mammals; among them Chinook salmon, halibut, sturgeon and whales. Such large, strong animals can only be caught if they are injured by a harpoon and hindered by ropes and floats, lose a considerable amount of blood and become exhausted by efforts to break free.

Size commands respect; a sturgeon can weigh 800 kilograms (1,800 pounds), a whale much more. A Nootka whaler showed his

Ceremonial paddle with raven painting on it, carved out of yellow cedar, made by Tlingit artist Reggie B. Peterson as part of his apprenticeship. The handle is modeled on a soul catcher used by the shamans. (88 cm; ICC)

Next to it, a Haida canoe paddle from the 19th century. (150 cm; MOA)

Upper right: A Halibut hook made of yew wood, bent by means of a steaming technique and then hardened. The bone barb is attached by means of a cedar bark string. Collected from the Haida, but of a type used by the Makah. (16 cm, MOA)

Lower right: A Haida halibut hook adorned with the figure of a chief wearing a potlatch hat engraved with a frog. (31 cm, over 110 years old; MOA)

special reverence for the animal in his thorough preparation. A Makah man talked about his father: "Months before the whale hunt my father already started praying. He knew special prayer songs that gave him power and he had magical charms that he kept in a secret place and didn't show to anyone. Sometimes he swam to the cliff beyond the surf, diving and spouting water like a whale; he made us believe that he was a whale to show that in his heart he was good." A man needed all the spiritual power he could get in order to lead his men in a whale hunt. And when the whale has been struck by the harpoon, he is asked to swim toward the shore. "Our people will welcome you," says the whale hunter to the spirit of the great animal. "We will sing and dance and decorate your great body with feathers." Perhaps the whale will understand and allow itself to be pulled to shore. Although the Nootka whaler went to the hunt with a different attitude than did Captain Ahab, who sought unholy revenge—and not every whale is the equal of the enormous and cunning sperm whale Moby Dick—the whale hunt was never without considerable danger. Many boats did not return home. If, however, the hunt was successful, the whaler and his crew were given great recognition. The grey whale, reaching a length of about 14 meters (46 feet), was hunted more than any other type of whale. To test their courage, young whalers sometimes tried to hunt the rarely attainable killer whale.

Hunting and Gathering

About 85% of the food consumed by coastal people came from the oceans and rivers, of which fish and sea mammals made up the largest part, while shellfish such as oysters, mussels, and clams, as well as sea urchins, starfish, and octopus made up the smaller part. Such a one-sided protein-rich diet appears to be not completely nourishing, especially for children, and some communities developed special nutritional rules for children.

Fruits and vegetables were, in terms of quantity, purely supplemental, a highly welcome addition to the diet, but strictly seasonal and subject to great regional variation. The Gitksan were familiar with 20 different types of berries, but of all available types of nuts, they gathered only hazelnuts. The Kwakiutl were fond of the roots of a particular type of clover. Wild onions, cow parsnip such as "rhubarb," the sweet inner bark of hemlock, or the bulbs of the camass plant helped to vary the menu. Berry patches and shellfish beds in the coastal waters were reserved for use by a particular family or village. Gathering itself was generally the work of the women, although boys and girls also helped. Once a particular berry was sufficiently ripe to be harvested, the entire household or village would travel to the site, erecting temporary shelters and sometimes staying for several days.

Fresh shellfish, various edible sea weeds, as well as fresh meat from the hunter's pouch, were particularly valuable as winter food. Waterbirds such as teal, widgeon, pintail, mallard and other wild

ducks, as well as geese and grouse, were welcome on the spit, but their feathers were not greatly valued. Most land animals were hunted or trapped not only for the meat, but also for their skins and fur: beaver, ermine, marten, mink, otter, lynx, red and silver fox, timber wolf; brown, black and grizzly bears, as well as deer, big horn sheep and mountain goats filled the long list of land animals. Preference and availability was, as always, regional.

Eating and Drinking

During the summer and autumn the two daily meals usually consisted of fresh food, such as raw, cooked or fried fish, cooked shellfish, berries and water. The women were skilled in preparing the apparently monotonous fish staple in dozens of different ways. Food had to be preserved to last over the winter and into spring. To that end, the various types of fish—principally salmon—were cleaned, filleted and hung over a large wooden rack. On sunny days, especially in the south, the fish was air-dried; in the north and during rainy weather, it was dried in the smoke hut. Fish roe and the candlefish were pressed in special oil presses to render their valuable oil. Fish and whale oil was not only used to dip fish and meat pieces at meals, but was also considered a gourmet drink. Water and berry juices alone were considered insufficient to serve as festive drinks. The pressed roe was worked into flat cakes and preserved by air-drying or smoking, or was turned into siwash, a delicacy similar to cheese. For gourmets, there was slightly gamey roe and fish heads—a great pleasure for the palate and the nose. A village otherwise concealed in a hidden bay could not be missed downwind during the fishing and drying season.

47

Raven and Man. A spoon made of mountain goat horn, carved in two pieces, and decorated with haliotis inlays. Haida. (25 cm; NMM)

Two bears in double profile holding a bowl shaped like an eagle's beak. Alder wood, haliotis, carved approximately 1895. (38 cm; SJM)

Page 46: Far left is a Haida ceremonial bow made of yew and decorated with a killer whale motif. It was collected around the turn of the century (125 cm; NMM). To the right is a Tsimshian bow painted with a bird motif, collected in Port Simpson in 1853. (152 cm; NMM)

Commerce and Trade Goods

Prehistoric finds show that there was, from a very early time, an active trade along the entire west coast and into the interior, a system of trade that probably expanded during the historic period. The Tlingit traveled as far as Puget Sound with their famous Chilkat blankets (photo Nr. 16) in order to barter them for dentalia snails, haliotis shells or to trade them for slaves. With their Athapaskan neighbors to the northeast, they traded fish oil for caribou and elk skins or for whole pieces of clothing. The Haida were known for their canoes and the Niska-Tsimshian for their candlefish oil, which was traded as far south as the California coast and east into the plateau region. The Nootka offered waterproof hats and baskets in addition to whale oil and slaves, and the Coast Salish traded basketry and blankets woven out of mountain goat and dog hair.

The Chinook, who lived at the mouth of the Columbia River, were especially skilled traders. For the purpose of trade, they developed a commercial language, a sort of lingua franca, which consisted of Chinook and Nootka words. Later, during the historic period, it was augmented with French and English words to produce a vocabulary of 700 to 1,200 words.

Cedar, a Limitless Raw Material

The heavily forested Northwest Coast inevitably made wood the most important raw material. Merely having a great deal of wood available,

The Coast Salish were known for their rugs made of the woolly hair of mountain goats and of the hair of dogs bred for this purpose. The breed of dog is now extinct. Note the infant strapped to a cradle board next to the Clallam women. Oil painting by Paul Kane, 1847. (ROM)

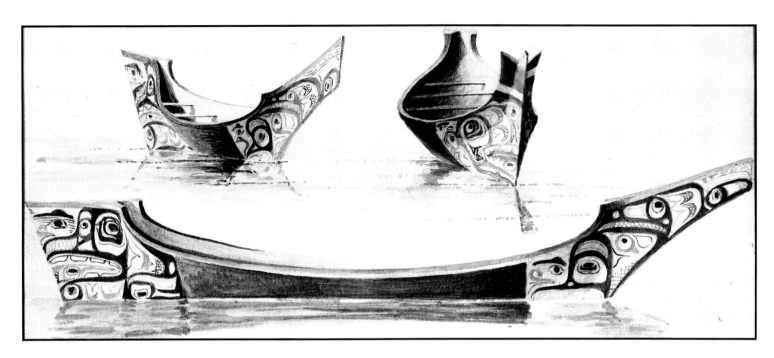

Studies by Paul Kane of the northern type of canoe with carved and painted bow and stern. (ROM)

The American mountain goat provided the Indians with the necessary raw material for Chilkat blankets, namely their spinnable hair. The horns were made into spoons.

however, does not guarantee the impressive degree to which the Indians of the Northwest Coast developed the art of crafting objects in wood. Their carvings bear comparison worldwide.

The most important tree to the Northwest Coast Indians was the red cedar. "Cedar," though a utilitarian term, is a botanical misnomer, since the red cedar belongs to the Thuja family of cypresses. The Thuja trees are also known under the name arbor-vitae, the "tree of life," and the Western red cedar (Thuja plicata) appropriately as the "giant tree of life." The trees grow to a height of 70 meters (231 feet), with a diameter of 5 meters (17 feet), and can reach 1,000 years in age. The red cedar is not fond of cold climates, which is why it is not found north of the 56th parallel.

The red cedar was used in making totem poles, canoes and houses. The Indian wooden houses amazed even the earliest European visitors. In the north, the walls were constructed of vertical and in the south, of horizontal planks. The floors were wooden planking, as were the roofs, and the storage chests were made of bentwood—all of which was accomplished before saws were available. How was this possible? The answer lies in the ease with which the red cedar can be split. An Indian carpenter needed only an axe and wedges to make corner posts, support beams and planks of any size, and any number of wooden objects.

Since the red cedar is also a lightweight wood, it is especially suited to the building of canoes. Although a canoe was fashioned from a single tree trunk, the Northwest Coast canoes were not mere dugouts. Once the middle had been hollowed out, the side walls were softened with water heated by means of hot stones and widened by the insertion of crossbeams. Finally, the entire bow of the canoe was artistically carved and painted. In the north, the stern received the same treatment. The length of the canoe varied: A fishing and hunting boat that could be carried measured 5 meters (17 feet), compared to 10 meters (33 feet) for a family or trading boat, and up to 20 meters

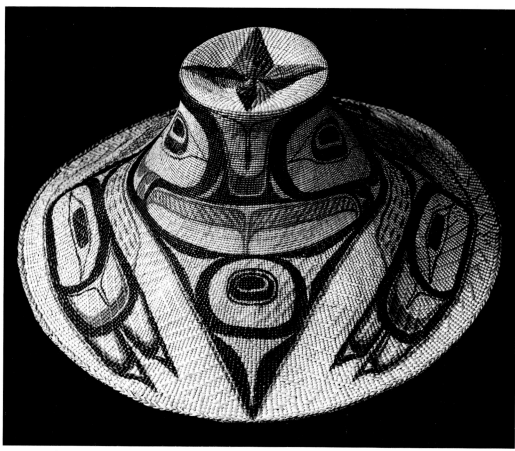

50

(66 feet) for a Haida war canoe.

The second false cedar, indigenous to the entire Northwest Coast, is called Alaska or Nootka cypress, as well as the yellow cypress. The first two designations are correct insofar as they indicate the tree's botanical link to the cypress family. The Nootka cypress, however, belongs to a different genus than the red cedar, and carries the name *Chamaecyparis nootkatensis*. The pale yellow color of the wood is the source of the name yellow cedar, by which the tree is generally known to the Indians. The trees reach the same considerable age as the red cedar, but do not grow higher than 45 meters (150 feet) or reach a diameter greater than 1 to 2 meters (2 to 6 feet). The dense, fine-grained wood is particularly well-suited for carving miniatures, such as small totem poles, but also for masks and relief carvings.

Indian people felled other conifers commonly found on the Northwest Coast for use as building material and firewood, among them Douglas fir (*Pseudotsuga taxifolia*), Western hemlock (*Tsuga heterophylla*) and Sitka spruce (*Picea sitchensis*). Alder, because it has no flavor, was carved into plates and bowls used for eating. Maple was best suited for spoons and shaman rattles; the flexible wood of yew trees was used for bows and fishhooks; and the hard wood of the wild apple tree was used to make wooden hammers and wedges.

Cedar and pine trees provided not only lumber, but also bark and roots, which were equally valuable as raw materials for making clothing and other utilitarian items. The inner bark of the red cedar, and above all the yellow cedar, proved to be especially useful for making baskets. During the transition from spring to summer, the women went into the forest, sought out young trees and spoke a

Watertight hat made of spruce roots, woven by Isabella Edenshaw (1858-1926) and painted by her husband, Charles Edenshaw (1839-1920), a famous Haida artist from Masset. The painting shows Raven in double profile. (about 40 cm; ASM)

This portrait mask is an example of the art of wood carving. The mask is either Bella Coola or Heiltsuk. (28 cm; NMM)

Haida ceremonial hammer. The soft stone is carved in the shape of a hawk with a whale in its beak. It is fastened to the wooden handle with cedar bark thongs. (68 cm; NMM)

prayer for the tree's soul. Then they notched the bark near the base, loosened it carefully and tried to tear a long strip of bark free, tearing upward. The inner, lighter bark was separated from the rough outer layer and then brought home to be used in various ways. The raw bark was transformed, for example, into a simple water ladle or a small canoe. Of much greater importance, however, was the prepared bark, which was beaten until it became a soft fiber. It was then separated into strips and bands of varying width. This fiber was one of the raw materials for coarser woven products such as mats, baskets and shawls. Often it was used in combination with other materials, such as fine, peeled spruce roots. Roots were well suited for the coil technique, which guaranteed a watertight weave. When using this method, the weaver works with two weft strands which are crossed over each other at each warp strand. The process results in a tighter weave than the less useful plaiting technique.

The Indians had few basic tools available for the crude work of felling trees and splitting and hollowing out logs, but the tools that were available appeared in several variations. Axes, hatchets, wedges, stone and wooden hammers, chisels and adzes comprised the basic set of carpenter's tools. The blades were made of nephrite, shell, horn and in rare cases of metal from parts of the wreckage of ships that washed up on the shore. In order to create detailed carvings, craftsmen also used knives with straight or curved blades, usually made from shells. Sharkskin was used as sandpaper. With the arrival of Europeans, the Indians immediately began making extensive use of metals of every type to improve their tools.

TLINGIT

The wildly romantic beauty of the Tlingit homeland is characterized by the glacier-torn coastal mountain range and, above all, by the countless islands of the Alexander Archipelago. Tlingit territory stretches from Yakutat Bay, the northernmost extent of the culture area of the Northwest Coast Indians, south to the Portland Inlet, a distance of more than 800 km (480 miles) by air. The Tlingit were as mighty and as proud as the grandiose country they inhabited. At the time of the first contact with white men, about 200 years ago, their people numbered 12,000 or more. The Russians, who were the first Europeans to move into Tlingit territory, could consider themselves fortunate that the combative Tlingit—after 1802—did not drive them out a second time.

The Tlingit are famous for their weapons, armor and helmets, but also for their impressive, colorful Chilkat blankets. Although it is thought that the origins of this textile art came from the Tsimshian, it was the women of the Chilkat Tlingit, who lived at the upper end of the Lynn Canal, who actually developed the twilled twining technique used to create the five-cornered blankets into an art form. It is not quite accurate to call it a "blanket," since it is really a ceremonial robe that is worn across the shoulders like a bishop's chasuble. In the traditional Chilkat dances, which dramatize myths, the dancer moves the edges of the blanket like wings. Anyone who has ever witnessed a Chilkat dance will never forget the spectacular scenery and the overall visual impact.

It is a wonder that the old customs of the Tlingit are still alive today. For one, these people nearly died out through diseases introduced by the Europeans—the 1920 census showed only 3,895 Tlingit still living. For another, they were subject to tremendous pressure to assimilate into the new dominant culture. First the Russians and their orthodox priests and later the Americans with their various Protestant missions tried to reform the "heathen savages" into "honest Christians." This process was abruptly discontinued with the discovery of gold near Juneau and in the Klondike region at the close of the 19th century. At that point the non-Indians who streamed into Tlingit territory hardly represented the best of white civilization. Discrimination against and exploitation of Native people increased. Some Tlingit saw the solution to these problems by furthering their own assimilation and fought for recognition as American citizens. To this end, nine Tlingit and one Tsimshian from Metlakatla founded the Alaska Native Brotherhood (ANB) in Sitka in 1912. All of the founders were members of the Presbyterian Church and strongly rejected all tradition, even their own native language. In 1922 the Tlingit became United States citizens. Subsequently the ANB several times successfully worked for recognition of land rights.

In the last 20 years the ANB and the Alaska Native Sisterhood, founded three years later, have stopped denying their native origins and now support many of the efforts to revive traditional culture. Between 1906 and 1971 not a single totem pole raised in Tlingit territory was celebrated with a potlatch. This was demonstratively changed when, on the occasion of a three-day potlatch, a 40-meter-high (132-foot-tall) totem pole was raised in Kake. Apparently, the old Tlingit culture has survived in some aspects. The language, for instance, has not died out, and is now being taught in the schools. The rules by which family relationships are determined, as well as those for ceremonial gift giving, have also survived.

The Tlingit are not only concerned with the preservation of their cultural identity. Their livelihood and continued existence in their ancestral territory is seriously threatened, particularly where their rights to the land and fishing are concerned. Until the passage of the dubious Alaska Native Claims Settlement Act (ANCSA) in 1971, their land rights were frequently confirmed, although over time they did lose massive tracts of land. With ANCSA, the U.S. government hoped to settle all remaining Alaska native-land claims. Aboriginal title to lands was extinguised and Alaska natives were compensated for these losses by means of newly granted tracts and money payments. Twelve regional native corporations were established with trust responsibility for the land and the power to invest the money in economic enterprises, for example, in fish and lumber businesses. A number of these corporations have already incurred debts and are likely to declare bankruptcy when they become subject to property taxes in 1992, as mandated in ANCSA. As of that year, the land may also be freely sold, so that a large-scale sale of native land is a distinct possibility when the corporations have to repay their debts. It is hoped that the 14,300 Tlingit with their economically successful SEALASKA Corporation will be spared this fate.

14   Especially impressive as examples of the art of mask making are the crown-like frontlets of the northern coastal people. A chief would wear one of these decorative headpieces during the dance to welcome his guests. The mask shown depicts what is presumably an eagle, below which is a human face. The mask is made of hard wood, haliotis, sea lion whiskers and eagle down; "fringe" is of ermine skins. (Mask 19 cm, extender 85 cm; SJM)

15   Harold Jacobs, a young crafts apprentice at the Southeast Alaska Indian Cultural Center in Sitka, poses in ceremonial clothing. He is wearing a wooden wolf hat, a thunderbird Chilkat blanket, and a silver nose ring. The wolf rattle he is holding, carved by Reggie B. Peterson, tells us that Harold Jacobs is a member of the wolf moiety.

16   The most famous blankets are those of the Chilkat Tlingit. The repetitive rectangular design elements and the very rare red color probably mean that it is an old Tsimshian blanket. (159 cm; NMM)

17   This replica of an eagle clan hat was specifically made for the museum by a Tlingit artist. It is made of haliotis and human hair. (27 cm diagonal; ASM)

18   This small bear figurine with its four "potlatch rings" was probably part of a larger headdress at one time. (Figure 18 cm; SJM)

19   The upper end of a talking stick, which was held by a chief on ceremonial occasions; with wolf's head and haliotis inlays. (166 cm; SJM)

20   Rattles also belonged to the insignia of a chief. This old raven rattle has two special features: First, a human face is carved onto the upright tail feathers and, second, the tiny human figure is holding two large mountain goat horns. (35 cm; MOA)

21   This basket, collected around the turn of the century, is a stunning example. It is woven of spruce roots and multicolored grasses. The blue color is created with huckleberries. (38 cm; ASM)

22   This photograph of a section of one of the four house posts that supported the roof beams of the eagle's nest house in Sitka shows the legendary young eagle who helped a girl to survive after an epidemic had killed her clan. The girl later became the ancestor of the Kaagwaantaan clan, which made the four 200-year-old house posts available to the Sitka National Historical Park on a long-term loan.

23   These two brothers, Harrry and Peter Johnson, supplement their income as Chilkat dancers, performing with the famous dance group in Haines, Alaska. Their costumes and masks are replicas of the originals.

24   Bear's head on a totem pole; Auke Bay, Juneau.

25   In the 1930s, the Stikine Tlingit moved to Wrangell, where they built a ceremonial house on the small island in the harbor. The house was ceremoniously opened in 1940. The painting on the front indicates it is a bear clan house.

26   The back wall inside the house is painted in a design based on a Chilkat blanket. The two house posts carved with killer whales and, on the right, with cuttlefish, are copies of old, decayed posts. They were added in 1985 and dedicated by means of a potlatch.

27   On another house post in the bear clan house in Wrangell, a large anthropomorphic bear appears to be protecting the figure of a human being, while a frog peers out of its mouth.

28   Aerial photograph of the McBride Glacier in Glacier National Park, Alaska.

29   The artist Nathan P. Jackson models the frontlet of his own raven moiety and a ceremonial button blanket. He carved the mask himself. Button blankets are considered the cheaper version of the Chilkat blanket. They are made of recut Hudson's Bay blankets and decorated with haliotis buttons. Visible in the background are the Tongass Narrows near Ketchikan.

▷   An old chief's hat, woven of fine spruce roots and decorated at the top with an ermine skin (about 1850). Each of the cylindrical rings is said to symbolize a potlatch hosted by the wearer of the hat, although the generally held theory that such rings are "potlatch rings" is controversial. The painted design could represent an eagle or the wealth-bringing sea monster Gonakadet. (61 cm; ASM)

14

18

19

25

26

TSIMSHIAN

According to tradition, the ancestors of the Tsimshian left their earthen lodges in the southern interior a long time ago, fleeing the long winters and frequent famines, to come to the paradisal Damelahamid. After overcoming many obstacles and fighting many battles they reached the "promised land" between the Skeena and the Nass Rivers, where they came to be known as the "People of the Skeena," on the "misty river." So goes the mythical history of the Tsimshian, who, in fact, are historically among the most recent immigrants to the Northwest Coast. They successfully drove the indigenous Tlingit farther to the north, the Haisla farther to the south, and they fought with the Heiltsuk over the coastal areas. Their territory included a large area whose boundary followed the Nass River to the southern shore of Portland Inlet and extended as far south as the Milbank Sound. The Tsimshian, numbering more than 10,000, were widely feared because of their aggressive war bands. They controlled the trade in eulachon oil, derived from the fish that returned to the Nass River in large numbers annually. When the Hudson's Bay Company opened a trading post in Port Simpson in 1831, the Tsimshian also assumed a dominant role in the fur trade and acted as agents to the neighboring peoples. It is not surprising that the chiefs of the Tsimshian villages acted like princes.

1857 was to be a fateful year for the Tsimshian. A decisive transformation occurred when a 25-year-old Anglican lay priest, William Duncan, arrived in Port Simpson with the exalted purpose of preaching the gospel to the "barbarian, even cannibalistic savages." Within a few months he had learned their language and so gained their respect. It was not long before four of the nine chiefs there allowed themselves to be baptized; the majority of the people followed their example. In 1862, Duncan, along with his group of converts, decided to leave the "den of iniquity," Port Simpson, in order to found a truly Christian community in the southern, abandoned Indian village of Metlakatla. Over the next 25 years, under his strict rule, this little community with an original population of 600, built the village up into a prosperous community with its own fish processing plant, school, brass band and police force. In 1887, after William Duncan quarreled with his superiors in the church and was unable to acquire additional land from the Canadian government for "his" Tsimshian, he emigrated together with 825 Tsimshian to southeast Alaska, where the United States designated the Annette Islands a reservation. The new Metlakatla was soon constructed and enjoyed a respectable prosperity, a fact which strengthened Duncan's reputation as an expert in the "civilizing" of Indians.

Until William Duncan's death in 1918, the history of the Metlakatla Tsimshian showed remarkable progress, although some community members no longer entirely agreed with Duncan. His memory is still revered, however, and his house is open to visitors as a museum.

Today, just as it was 100 years ago, the Metlakatla economy depends primarily on fishing, although the community is seeking to diversify. In addition to the cannery, the lumber mill offers temporary employment, since the sparse forestry allows for a harvest only once every eight years. A fish hatchery has been in operation since 1979. The tourist industry is still small, but it is constantly being developed. Unfortunately, these economic efforts are insufficient for the 1,400 inhabitants, many of whom are forced to seek a living away from the reservation, either in nearby Ketchikan or in Seattle, far to the south.

Other Tsimshian communities have had similar experiences, although none were influenced by personalities as strong as William Duncan. Nevertheless, they have fought hard for the rights to their land. In 1913 the Niska-Tsimshian filed the first land-rights suit brought by a Canadian Indian people against the Canadian government. Although they lost the case, the suit has continued in one form or another down to the present. Tsimshian people can now live in the hope that their rights may yet be vindicated, thanks to the development of international rights of indigenous peoples.

One cannot speak of the Tsimshian without mentioning 'Ksan. White men who had an eye for art were aware of the great beauty of the Northwest Coast Indian wood carvings during the early contact period. Somehow the Tsimshians were able to preserve their art work. In 1970 they reinforced their dedication to tradition by establishing an open-air museum called 'Ksan, a representation of a Gitksan village in about 1800, located near Hazelton. The first Indian art school in British Columbia also opened simultaneously inside the museum complex. The museum is the pride of approximately 10,500 Tsimshian living today. At the Northwest Coast Indian Art School, talented artists are trained in all techniques by instructors who are often recognized artists.

30   The shamans of the Northwest Coast utilized charms in their healing ceremonies. They were usually carved of bone or ivory in the form of a guardian spirit. The charms were either sewn on to clothing or worn around the neck. These little pelican figurines, attached to one another with a leather thong, form a rare charm which is considered to be quite old. It is made of bone and decorated with haliotis inlays. It was collected from the Tsimshian during the last century. (7 cm; NMM)

31   Another shaman charm, which was collected fully 100 years ago from the Niska on the Nass River. Carved of bone, it represents a salmon. (9 cm; NMM)

32   This drinking vessel is carved out of the tusk of a walrus and decorated with haliotis shell. The partially visible figure is probably an anthropomorphic bear. The cup originated in the same region as the salmon charm described above. (14 cm; NMM)

33   The apron of a Niska shaman consists of several pieces of leather sewn together with cedar bark thread and animal sinew and painted with ochre paints. Thirteen ivory halibut charms are tied onto it with cotton threads. Dog's teeth are fastened onto the bottom edge and deer hoofs are attached to the 10-cm-long (4-inch-long) leather fringes. (95 cm; NMM)

34   The Tsimshian may have been the first to make raven dance rattles. This example represents a widely disseminated model: On the back of a raven sits a man whose tongue is being pulled out by a frog, which is, in turn, being seized by a kingfisher. The underside of the rattle shows a hawk. "Underside" is incorrect insofar as this was the side which was on top when a chief held the rattle in his hand. (28 cm; ASM)

35   Several totem poles of varying antiquity have been preserved in the Gitksan village of Kitwanga. They are reminders of the exhibitions which Tsimshian chiefs made of their social rank and power, with traditional iconography. From the left: The mountain lion totem pole is more than 140 years old and shows, below the superimposed puma, alternately two wolves and two bears. The next is a wolf totem pole from 1895; in the middle, a female bear squats with two cubs at her feet. The subject is the mystical woman Xpisunt, who lived for a time among bears and bore twins who were half human and half bear. As the base figure, she is depicted in human form holding one of her children

in her arms. On the next post, dating from 1942, one of her bear children is attached above the bear mother Xpisunt; her second child once sat on top of the pole. The myth of Xpisunt is continued in the totem pole at right, known as the Bear Pole. The brothers of Xpisunt killed her bear husband and brought her and the twins home. Her children helped set bear traps and, consequently, all of their descendants were successful bear hunters. The figure of a wolf is fastened to the top of this 110-year-old pole; underneath it are Xpisunt and her twins, then two wolves and a bear. The fifth pole was erected in 1919. Its name is "On Which Raven Swung Himself Up," although Raven is missing from the pole and the figure of Axgawt has lost all of its original chiefly trappings, such as its copper plate.

36   Eagle's head on a totem pole in Kispiox. The pole is more than 100 years old.

37   View of the Nass River late in the afternoon near Old Aiyansh, in the heart of the land of the Niska. In the background is the coastal range.

38   The open-air museum at 'Ksan, near Hazelton.

39   Similar to other Northwest Coast villages, the new community centers are being modeled on traditional building styles. This is the longhouse of New Aiyansh, on which a thunderbird and several killer whales have been painted.

40   The Skeena River in autumn. This stretch is between Kispiox and Hazelton.

41/42   The Indian child between two cultures. A church in the village of Hagwilget, near Hazelton, is a symbol of the white world. The new ceremonial house in Kitwancool and the mythical Will-a-daugh with her wood worm child on a replica of an old totem pole symbolize the Indian tradition.

▷   This frontlet, from the Niska-Tsimshian village of Greenville located on the Nass River, shows a crouching bear. It is inlaid with colorful haliotis. (19 cm; MOA)

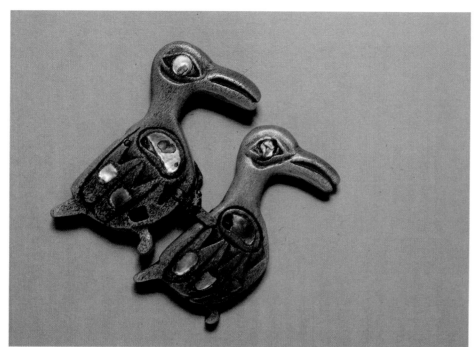

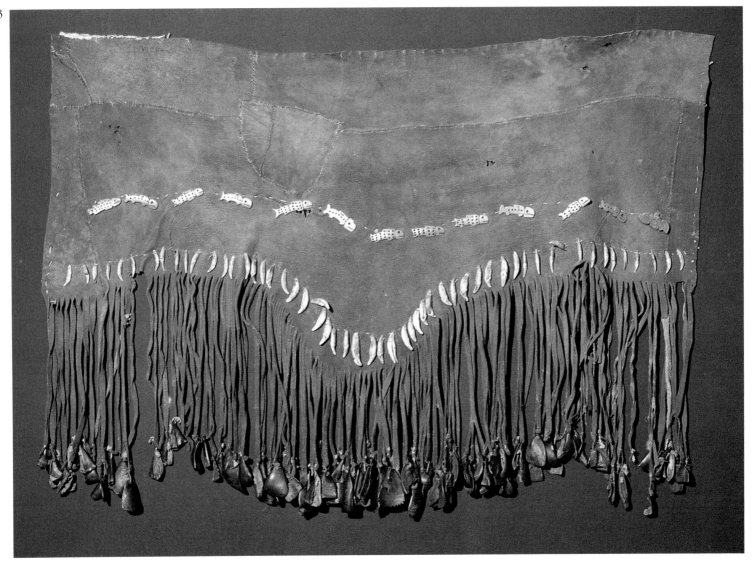

38

39

84

In 1921 the Nimkish chief Daniel Cranmer held an elaborate potlatch on Village Island. Later he talked about it proudly:

"Everyone admits it was the biggest potlatch in a long time. I am proud to say our people, the Nimkish, are ahead although we are only ranked in third place after the Kwakiutl and the Mamalelqala.

"So I am a big man in those days. Nothing now. In the old days, then the potlatch was my weapon, and I could call down anyone with it. All the chiefs say now in a gathering: 'You cannot expect that we can even get up to you. You are a great mountain.'"

RULERS AND SUBJECTS

The history of the social organization in Northwest Coast Indian communities is a complex one. Unraveling this social structure has been among the most difficult undertakings of anthropologists working with North American Indian people. A growing body of specialized literature has attempted to clarify and to define the differences and similarities within the culture areas. This has added to the complexity of the knowledge about the social organization. At the same time, a simplified and generalized description has become virtually impossible to attain. Therefore, this book can only provide a basic sketch of the various social systems, illustrated with examples.

A brief glance at our own social system can help clarify some basic concepts and contrasts. The social touchstone in western society is the nuclear family which, consisting of parents and children, combines two generations in a household. At the present time, the grandparent generation generally does not live in the same home. Except in the event of a rite of passage, such as a christening, confirmation, marriage or funeral, relatives do not assume an important role with regard to the nuclear family. Extended family members no longer have economic or political obligations to one another; these functions have been taken over by the economic system and political institutions—the city, county, state and even the political parties. Only among the influential upper-class families and members of the European nobility do family connections still play a role (for example, in marriages). This behavior, which is increasingly atypical for the majority of people, is based on class consciousness, and securing and consolidating wealth and power. It does, however, provide us with a useful parallel. The traditional Northwest Coast cultures are reminiscent of feudal times in Europe, insofar as they were clearly a class-conscious society with a class of nobles ruling over a large group of commoners who had no rights.

The Kinship System

The social system of the Indians of the Northwest Coast was organized vertically as well as horizontally. Definite rules governed family relationships. Unlike our system, the most important social unit was

A Haida chief's speaker's staff. An eagle, a raven with pointed ears and a wolf can be identified on the stick. By gesturing with the staff the speaker could emphasize certain words or sentences. (92 cm; VM)

not the nuclear family, but the so-called lineage, which included all persons related by blood who trace their descent either through the mother or the father. The chart below provides a model of a matrilinear lineage. In order to understand such a model, we begin at a starting point with Ego, the chief of the lineage. Belonging to the lineage in the generation of Ego's parents are his mother, who is still living, and her younger sister, as well as her deceased brother, formerly the lineage chief until his death. This role has been inherited by the eldest son of his eldest sister, who is Ego. In Ego's generation, we find his younger brother and two sisters belonging to the lineage, as well as the children of his mother's sister.

The children of the deceased chief belong to the lineage of the chief's widow. Ego's own children are members of his wife's lineage. The children of his older sister and those of his cousins, on the other hand, belong to Ego's lineage. The oldest son of this sister will succeed to Ego's position as lineage chief.

Another characteristic of the lineage system was the requirement that one's marriage partner had to be chosen from a different lineage. As a general rule, an aspiring lineage chief married the oldest daughter of his uncle, the one whom he would succeed as lineage chief. In this model, Ego's wife, under the matrilinear system, belonged to the lineage of her mother, so the marriage combined two lineages. This tie between two lineages, according to the rules of a matrilinear type of organization, was not considered a blood relationship; instead, it resembed a political union. In the noble classes and especially in the families of chiefs, such marriages were

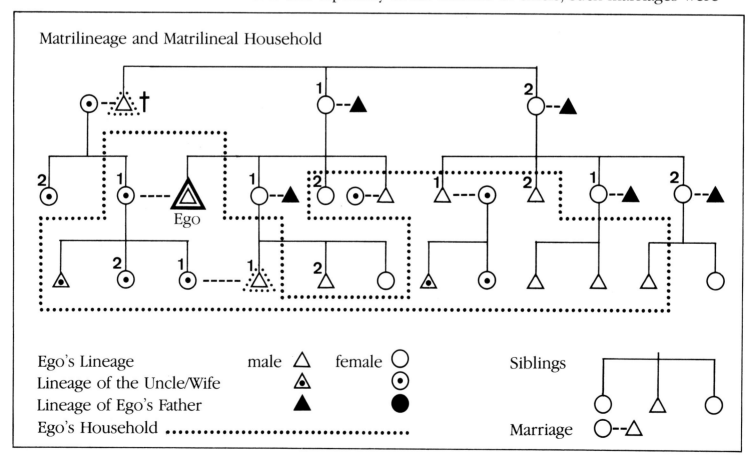

Matrilineage and Matrilineal Household

Ego's Lineage	male △	female ○	Siblings
Lineage of the Uncle/Wife	⊿	⊙	
Lineage of Ego's Father	▲	●	
Ego's Household ●●●●●●●●●●●●●●●●●●●●●●●●●●●			Marriage ○--△

carefully arranged to preserve or strengthen one's own power.

The model illustrates in an ideal and typical way the marriage between first cousins: Ego marries his mother's brother's oldest daughter and his younger brother marries one of her sisters. Both wives are from the lineage which is horizontally to the left of Ego's lineage. Ego's sister marries into the lineage of her father, namely the son of his oldest sister, assuming that her father is the chief of the lineage to the right. The chart could be continued horizontally to the left and the right with other lineages which are connected with each other by marriage. Ideally, then, all of the male members of Ego's lineage marry into the lineage of Ego's wife, and all of the female members of his lineage marry into the lineage of Ego's father. "Ideally" in this context means that this was the expected norm which, however, could not always be adhered to.

On the chart, the members of Ego's lineage who live in the same great house are enclosed by a dotted line. Not all the members of the lineage live in their own lineage house, although all male members do live there. Along with the position of chief, Ego has inherited his uncle's house, which has been his home since he was eight. The widow of his uncle has returned to the house of her brother. Ego's mother and her sister live in the houses of their husbands. All of the men of his generation live in Ego's house, as do the unmarried sisters, but not the two cousins. In the children's generation, age is an important factor. Small children live first in the house of their fathers. Boys who have reached the ages of seven or eight move in with an uncle on their mother's side, while the girls continue to live with their fathers. Except in the case of a "princess," as the oldest daughter of a chief is called, they do not move out until they marry. As stated, the princess will marry the nephew of her father. She will then stay in the house of her father, which becomes the house of her husband.

Among the northern coastal peoples there was an additional social grouping, namely the clan. Clans are created when several lineages are recognized as being related by tracing their mothers' line back through many generations to a common, mythical ancestor. The Tsimshian recognized four clans. The Tlingit recognized 12, which were further divided into two groups. One such tribal half is called a "moiety" by anthropologists. The Haida did not recognize clans. Their total of 45 lineages were divided into two moieties: the eagle moiety, which included 23 lineages, and the raven moiety, which had 22 lineages. The moieties and clans were referred to by the name of a crest animal, often called a totem animal in literature, a concept that is misleading, according to anthropologists. The Northwest Coast people, in any event, do not consider the ancestor of a clan to be identical with the crest animal, any more than a European views himself as the descendant of the crest animal of his hometown. The concept of the totem has survived, restricted to the Northwest Coast, in the term "totem pole," where it serves to distinguish these art works from similarly carved wooden stakes in other cultures worldwide.

The table below represents the clans and moieties of the northern people. The horizontal lines name those moieties and clans that are theoretically related to one another across territorial boundaries. A Tlingit of the raven moiety was related to a Haida eagle-person, to a Niska raven-person and a Niska eagle-person, and so on. This type of relationship was, however, quite weak and did not prevent warfare between people so "related." As the table indicates, these horizontal "relationships" were not always characterized by means of the same crest animals. A Haida raven was, therefore, not "related" to a Niska raven. In that event, the exogamy rules, which applied to clans and moieties as well as to lineages, would have permitted a marriage, although such marriages rarely took place.

Haida moieties	Tlingit moieties	Tlingit: 12 clans	Gitksan Tsimshian: 4 clans each	Niska, Coastal and southern Tsimshian 4 clans each
eagle	raven	frog goose owl raven salmon sea lion	frog (raven) eagle	raven eagle
raven	wolf (eagle)	auk bear eagle shark whale wolf	wolf fireweed (killer whale)	wolf blackfish

A clan member had to find a marriage partner not only outside of his lineage, but also from a clan other than his own. The Tsimshian often found such a partner in their own village since, as a rule, all four clans were represented in each village. However, since the clan relationships spanned many generations, the clans, or moieties, were not limited to a single village. Related clan members could be found in other villages. A Tsimshian had ties to his clan, but his unqualified loyalties were to his village, which was composed of several lineages. If war broke out between two villages, it could happen that a warrior of the victorious village could take a prisoner who turned out to be a member of his own clan. Since it was prohibited to enslave a member of one's own clan, he simply traded his prisoner for a prisoner taken by a comrade with whom he did not share clan membership.

An individual, therefore, had loyalties and duties within his lineage, as well as within his clan or moiety. In general, these responsibilities did not conflict, but complimented each other. The lineage provided the basic living and working arrangement: It possessed the rights to fishing grounds, food-gathering places and hunting areas. In short, lineage provided the basic organization for economic activity. The clan or the moiety had certain duties to fulfill with regard to another clan or moiety. In Tlingit society, for example, one moiety helped the other in the building of a new house, or assumed the ceremonial duties when a member of the other moiety died.

The Class Structure

Horizontally structured societies with relative groups living parallel to each other were rather common in North America. It is only in the Pacific northwest culture area that it was combined with a vertical system incorporating two to three classes, a situation which contrasts sharply with the standard image of the egalitarian Indian living in harmony with his fellow men and with all of creation. The social status hierarchy is, in fact, the most striking aspect of Northwest Coast societies. All lineages and other social groupings were structured hierarchically and divided into the two classes: nobility and commoners. In some communities, the nobility was further divided into one class of families with the right to a position of chief and another class of nobles who did not possess this right. The head of a lineage or village is given various names in the specialized literature; "chief" being the most inappropriate of all, since tribal societies such as those existing in the plains culture area were unknown. Among Plains Indians, the leadership function of a chief was associated with functions other than those generally associated with Northwest Coast tribal leaders. The most appropriate general term would appear to be "head." The literal translation of the Tlingit term for such a person is "head of household," "master of the house" or "wealthy man." These all point to specific attributes of the position—the lineage lived in a single large house and the chief was the wealthiest of all the household's members. However, the terms say little about the social-political power of the chief.

Within the lineage, the chief's position of virtually absolute power was inherited and was jealously guarded within the chief's family. All of their efforts were aimed at securing and increasing possessions and privileges, either by means of advantageous marriages or through conquering new territories through warfare. The chief managed the fishing places and hunting and gathering areas for the group and was responsible for the successful accomplishment of those economic activities which were most vital to the community's survival. He affirmed the rank of those within his lineage and on rare occasions carried through advancements for deserving warriors, canoe builders or artists. The hierarchical system allowed for limited social advancement: this was less the case in the north and more common in the south. Insofar as the number of noble positions was absolutely set, a superfluous member of a noble family could find himself descending to the level of commoner. Among the Nootka, this was often the fate of younger sons of a chief in instances where the older sons already occupied all available noble positions.

In order to better visualize the vertical social system we will take a closer look at the Southern Kwakiutl. They were subdivided into 13 regional communities ("tribes") which, among themselves, were strictly organized in a hierarchy. Ranking was connected to the size of the population of the regional groups. That, in turn, was directly dependent on available resources—the regular return of fish to the rivers, which was the prerequisite for sustaining a large community.

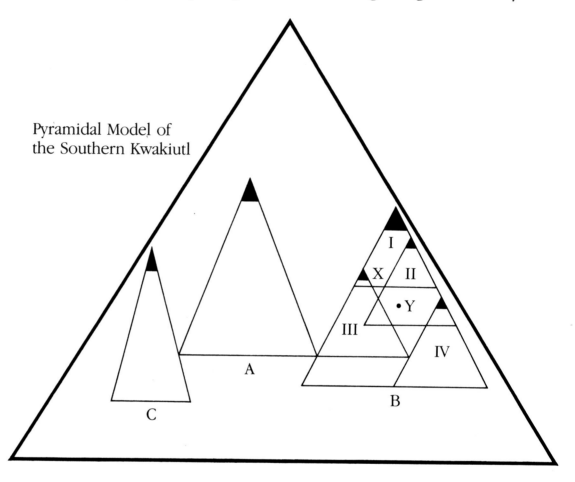

Pyramidal Model of
the Southern Kwakiutl

Each regional community consisted of a number of numaym, the term for the Kwakiutl concept of relative groupings, similar to lineage. The numaym were ranked among themselves, assuming from six to 42 hierarchically organized ranks. The hierarchical system of the entire Kwakiutl community can be represented schematically as a series of pyramids.

Regional community A was more highly ranked than B, and community B ranked higher than C. This meant that the chief of regional community A was at least theoretically head of all Kwakiutl regional communities. Within the regional community, the only person who could become regional chief was the head of the highest-ranking numaym. The overlapping of the pyramid signifies, for example, that Chief X of middle-ranking numaym B-III held a higher position within the regional hierarchy than lower-ranking member Y of the numaym

Tlingit warriors were reputed to be fearless in close fighting. This bone dagger with a raven head may be 200 years old. (38 cm; SNHP)

B-II, even though numaym B-II ranks higher than B-III. When the individual numaym came together each winter in the winter village, their ranks and the ranks of each individual were strictly adhered to. If doubts arose, the ranks were publicly documented and confirmed by means of a potlatch. On that occasion, the numaym myth was recited. It told of the exploits of the ancestors and provided precise information about the relationship of the numaym members to one another, as well as to their respective ranks.

Rank, as well as class membership, was determined by means of a bilateral descent system. A Kwakiutl man could freely determine whether he wished to pass his rank and possessions patrilineally to his firstborn son or matrilineally through a daughter to her son. The noble class had a preference for passing on the chief's position within a numaym through patrilineal succession. It was not, however, only succession which assured the chief's family the position of power. The sphere of influence could also be increased through marriage, since the exogamy rule required that a marriage partner be sought outside of one's own numaym, making an association with another numaym possible.

It was desirable for a nobleman to marry a woman of equal rank. In order to emphasize their elevated positions and the wealth associated with them, many chiefs allowed themselves several wives. With each marriage, a substantial bride price had to be offered to the prospective father-in-law. The father-in-law, in turn, would repay it over a period of time as evidence of the high rank of his daughter.

Those rights that were tied to rank, generally termed privileges, were diverse in nature. In addition to rights that were important to the numaym, such as rights to specific fishing and gathering places that were considered the possessions of the chief, a privilege could determine the value of possessions; give someone the right to be called by a certain name; permit the use of a certain design in tatoos or in the decoration of the house; or carry the right to perform a particular dance or wear a particular mask. The value of these privileges also had ranks, and the number of privileges was significant: Whoever owned one or several important privileges was a nobleman, while a commoner was one who owned none or totally unimportant privileges. While the nobles were clearly gradated as to rank, the hierarchy of the commoners was less noticeable. The separation between low-ranking nobles and high-ranking commoners was not always clear either, a fact which made social advancement a possibility, but could also lead to a loss of noble status.

91

Warriors and Slaves

In each Northwest Coast Indian community lived a number of slaves and their children, who made up the lowest level of this class system, extraordinary for a North American Indian people. They made up between 15% to 25% of the population. From the Indian point of view, they were not part of human society, but represented material goods. The majority were taken from their villages during military expeditions and enslaved. In order to hinder their escape, they were sold or traded for other slaves to people who lived a great distance away. Enslavement brought disgrace upon the victim as well as his entire lineage, so that the family of a slave, especially one of a high rank, made an effort to purchase his freedom. If they were successful, a special purification ritual was performed to remove the stigma of having been a slave, or at least to minimize it.

As possessions, slaves were primarily a source of prestige. In order to make a display of his wealth, a chief might sacrifice a slave or set one free; both actions would increase his standing. Coincidentally, slaves appear to have served an economic function as workers and as trade goods. They were made to perform the most menial

chores and lived on the leftovers of their masters. Since the majority of slaves were women and children, however, the economic gain from their labor, on average, exceeded the effort in keeping them by very little. It nonetheless appears to have been worthwhile for the noble classes to keep slaves. In times of need, one could sell them in exchange for food or let them starve first. Of course, during hardships the Nootka chiefs did not hesitate to deport even commoners to other less-needy communities.

The mortality rate among slaves was consequently quite high and villages were forced to undertake military expeditions repeatedly to acquire new slaves and goods, as well as to capture new territories. In contrast to most other North American people, the wars of the Northwest Coast Indians were quite cruel. The warriors were general-

This oil painting by Paul Kane depicts an attack on the Clallam village of Iehnus (Yennis) by the Nootka. The village was protected by high palisades. In the background, on the other side of the Strait of Juan de Fuca, the mountains of Vancouver Island are visible. (1847; ROM)

Page 93: In defending Sitka in 1804 against the attacking Russians, the Tlingit war chief Katlean wore this raven helmet. It is made out of a piece of wood covered with bear skin. The eyes are copper. (SJM)

Tlingit war dagger. The blade was ground out of a file, the handle is carved cedar with haliotis inlays. (51 cm; NMM)

The wooden armor of a Tlingit warrior with the symbol of his clan. (53 cm; SJM)

92

ly low-ranking young men of the noble class who practiced their profession in the late summer, after the salmon fishing season ended. They were well-trained, brutal in battle and were not permitted to display any emotions. Enemies who were killed were decapitated so that their heads could be displayed publicly as trophies. The battles were well-prepared and cunning and tactics were readily used. An attack on a village would occur at dawn, and it would not cease until virtually everyone in the attacked village had been killed. Vendettas and feuds were also widespread. The decimation of Northwest Coast people through European diseases and the new white masters put a stop to these violent power struggles in the 19th century. The potlatch was substituted for warfare: One's rival for positions of power were now fought with possessions.

94

The famous photographer Edward S. Curtis persuaded Hamasaka, the chief of the Kwakiutl at Fort Rupert, to pose in his ceremonial robes. In his left hand he holds a speaker's staff, in the right a dance rattle. Draped around his shoulders is a typical button blanket with symbolic potlatch coppers. (GA)

The Potlatch

The unique institution of potlatch has as its primary purpose the repeated and public reaffirmation and validation of both the horizontal lineage system and the vertical hierarchy of rank. It is really a gift-giving celebration, expressed by the Chinook concept of potlatch, which means "giving." When the position of chief is passed to a successor, the potlatch serves to validate the successor as the legitimate heir. The lineage chiefs, therefore, invited other lineage chiefs with their linear relatives to a feast which lasted several days and where the guests were assigned seats strictly in accordance with their social positions. The host and members of his family recited myths and genealogies in which the succession would be clearly laid out. The guests were served delicacies and given generous gifts, gradated in value according to the recipient's place in the hierarchy. By accepting the gifts, the guests recognized the legitimacy of the presumptive heir to the position of chief in the lineage of the host.

This brief description of a succession potlatch reflects a clear understanding of the function of the potlatch in the various Pacific Northwest cultures that does not exist in actuality. This ignorance results from a lack of information transmitted from the pre-contact period. What little information is available provides evidence that even during the early times, variations in the potlatch system must have existed along the coast corresponding to the social, economic and ecological differences between Northwest Coast cultures. At the same time, during the colonial era and especially in the course of the 19th century, the potlatch changed considerably, a fact for which the decimation of the population, as well as an increase in European mass-produced goods, is responsible.

The original function may well have been the exchange of food items for so-called potlatch goods in order to help a suffering community through a famine. The potlatch precisely documented the exchange of goods, as much with a view to future trade relations as to a reversal of economic circumstances, should the helping community find itself in trouble while the one now being helped had a surplus. As mentioned earlier, the Indians of the southern coastal region had to deal with a food supply that was not always dependable, while the strictly hierarchical societies in the north, where environmental conditions were more stable, ran less risk of famines.

Furthermore, the nobility did not have to suffer from starvation, but the slaves and commoners were all the more exposed and, finally, one had the option of ambushing and raiding neighboring villages. In this environment, the potlatch more closely served the purpose of justifying claims to positions of power. This judicial-political function was probably its single most important purpose along the entire Pacific Northwest coast. These repeated, public testimonials to the validity of the social structure served in place of written records in pre-literate society.

Special events of social significance in the lives of individual people and in the community as a whole gave rise to a confirmation

This photograph, taken around the turn of the century, shows the family of a Niska chief from Gitlakdamix during a potlatch with all of their potlatch goods. (PM)

potlatch. After the birth of a noble child, a potlatch would be held on the occasion of the naming of the child. During an individual's childhood, the father or matrilineal uncle would hold potlatches at regular intervals in order to confirm the legitimacy of the child's future rank. Another occasion could be a marriage, where the potlatch served as public testimonial of the new alliance created by the marriage.

The construction of a new house was also an occasion for holding a potlatch; the distribution of potlatch gifts resembled payment for

contributed labor. The raising of a totem pole led to a memorial potlatch to honor desceased ancestors. The death of a chief required not only appropriate mortuary rites, but also a potlatch presenting his successor.

The validation purpose that underlies most potlatches also served the needs of the chiefs and noble classes to lend legitimacy to the unequal distribution of wealth and power through ostentatious feasts, which conferred social prestige on the hosts. According to the sociological laws, this ceremony created a balance of power and prestige which helped to minimize internal social tensions. The commoners formed an admiring audience and simultaneously functioned as public witnesses when two noble families were engaged in potlatching. The strong hierarchical social structure and these often lavish potlatch feasts justify the term: "aristocracy" for the lineage, and "principality" for a larger village community, although the image of the Northwest Coast nobility does not exactly correspond to European feudal conditions.

Before European contact and continuing until about 1785, there were evidently fewer potlatches held than was the case in later times. The first serious shocks to the traditional social system occurred during the so-called fur trading period, from 1785 until approximately 1860. The Hudson's Bay Company, which was first a British and later a Canadian trading company, established a series of trading posts along the length of the coast. New Indian communities established themselves around these outposts. The precise rank of each group subsequently had to be established by means of many potlatches, since the colonial government had effectively put an end to warfare as a means of determining the respective ranks of villages.

The gravest social upheaval came about through the decimation of villages (which were sometimes reduced to 10% of the original population) by measles and small pox, introduced to the area by Europeans. For lack of appropriate heirs, conflicts arose over the assumption of hereditary rights, especially to the higher-ranking positions. The established ranks remained in place, but often could not be assumed by those with heirship rights to them—people with a clearly legitimate claim by birthright. Even the aristocracy was not immune to the European diseases. A new variation to the institution of the potlatch developed—the so-called rivalry potlatch. This variant has to be considered in combination with the changes in their economic system which Northwest Coast Indians experienced in the 19th century. An increasing number of white people were settling on the west coast, bringing with them a money economy and the mass production of material goods. Indians now had the opportunity to acquire paying jobs and to purchase European goods with their income. Even commoners could, in a short time, become newly rich in comparison to members of the noble class who stayed at home. It follows that an increasing number of European goods, such as wool blankets, cookware and dishes, tools, sewing machines and other products were accumulated and given away at potlatches as the newly rich aspired to the unoccupied ranks of highly placed nobles.

If two rivals competed for one such noble rank, one of them had to, as in the earlier times, establish his claim with a validation potlatch. He would announce a potlatch for a particular time, inviting his rival with all of his relatives. Up to the day of the potlatch, the village of the host amassed vast amounts of goods and food to provide gifts and a feast for the guests. The rival could do one of two things: he could accept his host's superior wealth and with it his legitimate claim to the contested rank, or he could announce a reciprocal potlatch at which he would try to outdo his rival by distributing an even greater number of goods.

The concept of credit was also taken over from the European economic system, insofar as the members of the host's community lent their chief the potlatch goods at a high interest rate. Repayment was expected within one year, although there was never a debt foreclosure. The debtor who "defaulted" lost prestige or had to pay higher interest. Credit was not given with the intent of earning a profit, as in today's system, but it was intended to lead to a right to a higher rank for the lender. Among the most important potlatch goods at the time were the wool blankets sold and traded by the Hudson's Bay Company. These blankets were the scale against which other articles of value were measured. They were collected by the dozens, hundreds and even thousands and distributed at potlatches without ever being considered for their original purpose, that of giving warmth. Potlatch goods were not used in daily life, but were specially stored away.

Toward the end of the last century there was an "overheating" in the potlatch system, when rival potlatches became destructive. As competition escalated, rival potlatch hosts would take the last measure to humiliate their opponent by breaking the coppers, hammered sheets of raw copper each measuring about 75 cm (30 inches). A copper was something like a bank note of very high value, worth several thousand blankets. By breaking one of his coppers with a ceremonial hammer or by throwing it into the fire or into the ocean, the host excused all debts owed him. This act demonstrated that he was so wealthy that he was not dependent on the repayment of debts.

This spectacular form of potlatching was a thorn in the side of the Canadian government, which under a general policy of "civilizing" the native people, made it illegal to hold potlatches. The prohibition, which lasted from 1884 until 1951, did not prevent Northwest Coast Indians from holding potlatches. They were often held in secret, although the participants were sometimes caught and punished with jail sentences and confiscation of the potlatch goods. Especially attractive coppers or masks were often sent to museums. The Indians, however, never forgot the individual to whom these valuable items had last belonged. As long as the items were preserved safely in the museums, they gained additional value in the eyes of the Indians and continued to be exhibited and given away at illegal potlatches in the form of credit slips. Recently, many of the confiscated potlatch goods have been returned to their respective villages; some can now be seen in the new local museums.

97

Haida copper with etched and painted bear motif. The copper plate is more than 100 years old. (74 cm; MOA)

Page 96: Replica of the Yaadaas totem pole, the original of which stood in the Haida village of Old Kasaan. This copy was carved in 1978 by the Tlingit artist Tommy Jimmie. At the top is the village watchman, followed by Raven Yel in both his human and animal forms. At the bottom is a crouching bear eating an unidentified animal. (SNHP)

HAIDA

The Queen Charlotte Islands were first settled more than 9,000 years ago. The first people to inhabit them had to cross the sea between the mainland and the archipelago. This was no mean feat, since the Hecate Strait, which separates this group of islands from the rest of the Northwest Coast, is from 45 to 130 kilometers (27 to 78 miles) wide. The archipelago encompasses approximately 150 islands, with Graham and Moresby Islands making up most of the 9,033 square km (3,613 square miles). Geologists have determined that the Queen Charlotte Islands are part of the tertiary coastal range originally located in the South Pacific and were pushed into their present location by shifting continental plates. In addition, they experienced virtually no glaciation. This explains some of the unique plant and animal life that sets the islands apart from the mainland. All of the mammals and three species of birds are unique to the islands, and several plants are also found only in distant parts of the world, such as Japan and Ireland.

In 1774, when the Spanish explorer Juan Pérez Hernandez made contact with the Haida, followed four years later by the Englishman James Cook, there were more than 6,000 people living on the islands. There were also 3,000 Kaigani Haida living on the southern islands of the Alexander Archipelago. The Haida were more severely stricken by measles and small pox than were other Northwest Coast people; they came close to extinction. They lost more than 90% of their original population and, by 1915, only 558 Haida remained alive. They have since overcome this low point and their population has again begun to increase. Today there are 1,600 Haida living on the Queen Charlotte Islands; another 700 live outside of their homeland.

Due to the isolation imposed by the environment, Haida culture is extraordinary in various aspects. It represents a strikingly singular development of the cultural elements that define Northwest Coast Indian society. The Haida were reputed to be, for example, the best canoe builders, and their totem poles, in the form of mortuary poles, were unique. During the historical period, they became famous for their equally unique carvings in argillite, a gray-black stone.

One of the most noticeable stylistic elements of Haida totem poles is that the head of a figure is nearly always the same size as the body. The eyes of the figure are also quite large. In addition, the carving is done like a relief, so that the shape of the figures is emphasized considerably less than Tlingit or Kwakiutl art. The extraordinary beauty of Haida artworks already attracted scholars and collectors during the last century. Thanks to people such as the geographer Georges M. Dawson and the ethnographer Charles Newcombe, there are several photographic and cartographic records still in existence which give an insight into the deep impression Haida villages, with their innumerable totem poles, must have made on the first white men. One of these villages was Ninstints on Anthony Island. When Dawson visited the island in 1878, the village was abandoned and the houses and poles had begun to collapse. A quarter of a century later Newcombe attempted to identify precisely all of the houses and poles of the village in order to create a historical record.

After World War II, Marius Barbeau of the National Museum of Man in Ottawa, visited the Queen Charlotte Islands to determine how much could yet be saved from ruin. His inspiration was converted into action in the mid-fifties by a team from the University of British Columbia in Vancouver and the Provincial Museum in Victoria. With the blessings of and cooperation from the Haida, archaeologists studied the Ninstints and other villages. Twenty-three totem poles, whole poles or parts of them, were transported to various museums for restoration and preservation. Some of the originals are on display at the Provincial Museum in Victoria, where John Smyly, a member of the team, has constructed a model village to give visitors an impression of the impact of a Haida village at its cultural peak. His prototype was not Ninstints but the equally magnificent village of Skedans (Koona).

Haida artist Bill Reid worked with the team from the beginning. We have him to thank not only for reconstructing several Haida houses and totem poles, which are on display in the open-air museum adjacent to the Museum of Anthropology in Vancouver, but also for the renaissance of Haida as well as all of Northwest Coast native art. The degree to which this art has found recognition worldwide is apparent in the November 27, 1981, UNESCO decision to add the ruins at Ninstints to the list of World Heritage sites worthy of preservation.

43 View from the sandspit on Moresby Island over Shingle Bay to the coast of Skidegate, located on Graham Island. The Queen Charlotte range is visible in the background.

44 Aerial view of Anthony Island, location of the ruins of the Ninstints. In the background left is Kunghit Island. (See photos 8-13.)

45 Swampy forest in Naikoon Provincial Park on Graham Island.

46 Only a few decayed totem poles remain of Skedans, located on Louise Island, southeast of Skidegate. An eagle on the mortuary pole is recognizable by its wing; its beak is missing.

47/48 The figure of a bear is vaguely visible on the remains of each of these mortuary poles.

49 In this image from Skedans, a killer whale on a mortuary pole is "biting" the trunk of a tree, while the figure above it, a bear, "grasps" a branch. The battle against nature appears to be hopeless.

50 The natives of the Queen Charlotte Islands, on the other hand, have won their fight for survival. Daphne Yeltatzie, from the Haida community of Masset, maintains the tradition of hanging halibut fillets from a ceiling grate to dry.

51 This ancient memorial post stands in Skidegate and is in danger of toppling. The base figure is a beaver with a bear cub between its ears.

52 This raven dance rattle, on which a kingfisher is pulling a man's tongue, was collected in 1878 on the Queen Charlotte Islands. Given the style of the rattle, however, it may have been made by the Tlingit and came into the possession of a Haida family through trade, an exchange of gifts on the occasion of a marriage or as spoils of war. (34 cm; MM)

53 The Northwest Coast Indians played games with a passion. The so-called stick game was one of the favorites. A participant could lose all his possessions in this guessing game. The Haida called the game "Ssin," which means maple, one of the types of wood from which the sticks were carved. The sticks shown are 13 cm (5 inches) long, and the rawhide bag contains 73 pieces. (NMM)

54 This small wooden figurine measures 23 cm (9 inches) and presumably represents a shaman who is wearing his face mask and is holding two sea otters. (MOA)

55 Next to the Museum of Anthropology in Vancouver is this Haida open-air museum. The poles were carved between 1959 and 1962 by Bill Reid (born 1920) with the help of Doug Cranmer (born 1927) from Alert Bay. They are new works modeled on the old poles on the Queen Charlotte Islands. At the base of the pole to the left is a bear with a cub between its ears, a frog in its mouth and a wolf between its legs. The original was in Ninstints and today is in the adjacent Museum of Anthropology. The great house front pole with the shark fin on top is patterned after a pole in Skidegate, as is the third pole with a beaver as the base figure (see photo 51). The double mortuary poles for a chief, far right, show a dogfish on the coffin front. The original is in Skedans.

56 Argillite totem pole from the last century. From top to bottom, there is a bear, a raven with a frog on its wing, the figure of a chief and a hawk with a killer whale in its talons. (36 cm; MOA)

57 Wooden bowl for ceremonial use in the shape of a raven lying down with a hawk's head protruding from its tail feathers. (32 cm; MOA)

58 A bowl for food in the shape of a frog. (23 cm; MOA)

59 Like the raven rattle mentioned earlier, this figurine was acquired on the Queen Charlotte Islands more than 100 years ago. Certain stylistic elements, however, indicate that it is of Heiltsuk origin. It is not known how the piece came into Haida possession. The figure might represent a mythical person riding on the water-blowing monster. It is likely that this is a curiosity made to be sold to white men. (41 cm; NMM)

▷ This mask is a very rare piece and difficult to identify. It was acquired in 1878 from the Haida on the Queen Charlotte Islands, but it may have originated elsewhere. The form of the lines in the design and the shape of the face resembles a Heiltsuk or even a Tsimshian mask. With regard to many of the art objects, there is doubt as to who should be credited for them: the people who created them, or those in whose possession they were found and who made use of them? (NMM)

43

44

45 ▽

46

47 △

48 ▽

51

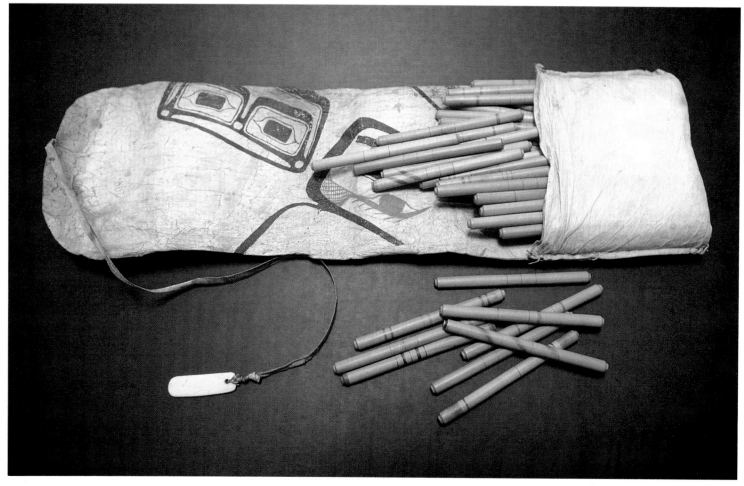

55

56

112

KWAKIUTL

The Kwakiutl are among the most researched people in North America. This, however, applies only to the Southern Kwakiutl, or true Kwakiutl, not to the Haisla or Heiltsuk, who belong to the same language group. The source of this extensive scientific interest may be found in the history of American anthropology. One of the originators of the discipline was Franz Boas (1858-1942), a German who conducted his research among the Kwakiutl between 1886 and 1931, while living on the Northwest Coast for periods. One of his undisputed achievements was his insistence that ethnographers who conducted field research should patiently collect extremely detailed data. Boas alone published more than 5,000 pages about the Kwakiutl. His efforts to create an empirical anthropology occurred during a time when Native Americans were viewed as a "vanishing race." His mission to collect detailed information about the last survivors was timely.

Less well known than Franz Boas was his most important informant, George Hunt, the son of an English father and a Tlingit mother. Although he grew up among the Kwakiutl at Fort Rupert, it is not known to what extent his English-Tlingit family influenced his perception of Kwakiutl culture. His help was invaluable in providing the ethnographic data with which Franz Boas worked, truly a flood of information: even Boas was unable to utilize it all. Boas was, finally, unable to present a fully rounded picture of Kwakiutl culture. Helen Codere, who studied under Boas, has stated that, in view of the mass of data collected, no one would have been capable of integrating all of it.

While we have a fairly clear idea of Kwakiutl material culture, all efforts have failed on the part of anthropologists to achieve consensus as to the enormously complex social order and religious practices. The same is true of the confusing developments that occurred in the potlatch system during the 19th century. The fact that these Indians have in recent years begun calling themselves Kwakwaka'waku, a more traditional name, while scholars continue to use the name Kwakiutl, reflects some of this confusion. The following discussion is therefore limited to a few relatively uncontroversial facts about the Kwakiutl.

The northernmost group, the Haisla, originally lived in two communities: Kitimat at the tip of Douglas Channel and Kitlope at the end of the Gardner Canal. At the time of first contact with Europeans, they numbered approximately 1,000; by 1918 the population had been reduced to 300 due to a series of epidemics. Since then, the population has again risen to its original number. Although the Haisla's access to coastal waters was blocked by the coastal Tsimshian, or perhaps because of the proximity of the Tsimshian, the Haisla were heavily influenced by Tsimshian culture, particularly that of the Gitksan. Like the Tsimshian, their social order was matrilineal, whereas the Southern Kwakiutl tended to a patrilineal system. Numerous Haisla are today employed by Alcan, in Kitimat, an aluminum smelter, which is visibly polluting the forests surrounding the inlet with fluorides.

The territory of the Heiltsuk Kwakiutl once extended from the 59th latitude to the Inlet River. They are often called Bella Bella, named after their main village, which is also the term to designate the Heiltsuk dialect. The original four groups had a combined population of approximately 1,800. For a time around the turn of the century, their numbers were quite low, but since then, their membership has again risen to 1,300. The Bella Bella carried on an intense commerce with their neighbors to the east, the Bella Coola, but warfare between them was also not uncommon. The Bella Coola, although a Salish-speaking people, were influenced extensively by the Kwakiutl. This cultural process worked in the reverse, and the Bella Bella were, in turn, influenced by their Salish neighbors. This process of cultural exchange can be observed along the entire Northwest Coast.

With an original population of 9,000, the Southern Kwakiutl were the most powerful of the Kwakiutl people, although they splintered into 28 smaller groups who carried on wars against each other. Their territory extended from Smith Sound south as far as Cape Mudge, where the Lekwiltok Kwakiutl had displaced the indigenous Comox Salish by 1850. Today there are 3,200 Kwakiutl living in 10 communities.

The Kwakiutl, now as in the past, are known for their immensely impressive art, created by such well-known artists as Willie Seaweed, Mungo Martin, Doug Cranmer and Tony and Richard Hunt. They have also maintained their historic reputation for aggression. The current battles, however, are for survival in an equally aggressive white society that threatens to destroy the environment of the Northwest Coast Indians.

60   Alert Bay is, without a doubt, one of the centers of the contemporary Kwakiutl community. This is where the Nimkish lived, once the third most powerful Kwakiutl group. Pictured is the current president of the village, Chief Pat Alfred, with one of his grandchildren.

61   During the renaissance of traditional Kwakiutl culture, a large ceremonial house was built at the initiative of the former chief, James Sewid. It is 15 meters (49 feet) wide, 21 meters (69 feet) long and 5.1 meters (17 feet) high. The center's opening on June 18, 1966, was planned to coincide with the Centennial of the Province of British Columbia. The front is decorated with an enormous killer whale, the door is protected by the figure of a guardian.

62   The Atlakin mask dance plays an important role in the ceremonial life of the Kwakiutl. Atlakim beings are forest spirits of the most diverse appearance. Their chief is Xamsalilala. He is the first to appear and summons the other 39 spirits, one after the other, into the ceremonial hall. This Xamsalilala mask, also shown on the dust jacket, was carved in the 1940s by the famous chief and artist Willie Seaweed (1873-1967), a Nakoaktok Kwakiutl from Blunden Harbor, located on the mainland opposite Port Hardy. Bill Holm dedicated an exhibition and a book with the title "Smoky Top" (Vulkan) to this famous chief and artist. (27 cm; MOA)

63   Of the four supporting posts of the ceremonial house in Alert Bay, the two posts in back are identically carved with the figure of the forest giantess Tsonoquoa with a thunderbird. The crossbeam represents the two-headed sea monster Sisiutl. The carving was done by a local artist, Henry Speck. The board wall, which shields the sacred part of the ceremonial house, depicts a thunderbird and a killer whale.

64   This mortuary pole with Tsonoquoa and the thunderbird stands in the cemetery at Alert Bay. It is one of the masterpieces of Willie Seaweed, who carved it in 1931.

65   The grizzly bear, depicted here with a human figure between its legs, is a favorite subject of Kwakiutl artists. In 1980 this totem pole was still standing on Main Street in Alert Bay. Unfortunately, its present location is unknown.

66   This 3.6-meter-tall (12-foot-tall) ancestral figure, carved from the wood of a red cedar, served as a house post in the interior of a Koskimo Kwakiutl house in Quatsino. The lower portion shows two slaves carrying a plank, which presumably served as the seat for a chief. A killer whale and coppers are depicted on the figure. (MOA)

67/68   These two house posts were collected in 1893 in Kitimat at the upper end of the Douglas Channel. They belonged to the Haisla Kwakiutl. (173 cm and 159 cm; MOA)

69   This soul catcher, representing the two-headed sea monster Sisiutl, belonged to a Haisla shaman from Kitlope, located on the Gardner Canal. If the shaman was successful in recovering the patient's lost soul during the healing ritual, he would keep it in the body of the small human figure, whose head is removable, and return it to the patient. (16 cm; MOA)

70   In this bentwood box, measuring only 32 cm (13 inches), a Haisla shaman from Kitimat stored his utensils. The lid is decorated with opercula, the "plugs" of a sea snail shell. (MOA)

71   Among the potlatch goods that were confiscated from the Nimkish in 1921 was this hawk mask, the guardian spirit of a chief. It was returned to the Nimkish and, since 1980, has been on exhibit in Alert Bay at the U'mista Cultural Centre. (See page 134.)

72   A Nimkish fishing boat is returning to the harbor at Alert Bay early in the morning. The downriggers for nets and lines are in a vertical position.

73   Bella Bella has been the main village of the Heiltsuk Kwakiutl for more than 100 years. It can only be reached by boat or plane. In contrast to most other Indian communities in Canada, the Bella Bella First Nation permits the sale of alcoholic beverages in its own liquor store.

74   Fishing is still an important industry for Northwest Coast Indians today. Because their fishing rights are not respected by the governments of Alaska or British Columbia, the Indians are forced to engage in expensive legal battles, which have even reached international proportions.

▷   This thunderbird frontlet, inset with haliotis shell, was the property of a chief of the Tlatlasikoala Kwakiutl, from Hope Island off the northern tip of Vancouver Island. He acquired it from the Bella Coola. (20 cm; MOA)

67

68

69

70

Once when the Gilutsau Tsimshian were threatened by a famine, they asked Wideldal, the great shaman of the Gitsemgalon Tsimshian, to use his prophetic gifts in their behalf to tell them if the eulachon would swim up the Nass River that year to save them. In view of the many gifts offered him, Wideldal was prepared to do this. He filled two vessels with river water and put half a dried eulachon in each one. Then he placed one vessel at the entrance of the house and the other at the back of the house. He said to the people: "When I start to dance around the house, watch the vessels carefully. As soon as any fish come to life, call out." He danced around the house three times, but neither fish moved. When Wideldal said: "If the fish do not come to life when I dance around the house for the fourth time, then you will starve." He had danced halfway around the house for the fourth time when one watcher called out: "The fish has come to life! He is alive!" Wideldal ended his dance and told the people: "Get your nets and set them, as there will be many eulachon." And this is what happened.

RAVEN AND SHAMANS

Religious concepts and practices were inseparable from the social and 133
economic realities of Northwest Coast people. Religious beliefs and
their expression through ceremonies were not limited to Sunday
mornings. Social and economic factors were too tightly interwoven
with religion to relegate it to a particular time or place, a condition
reminiscent of early European peoples. It is, therefore, not surprising
that the religion of the Northwest Coast Indians was as complex as
their social organization. There were no churches and no priests,
even a so-called God was unknown. Religion varied from one culture
to another, and it even assumed highly individual aspects in some
cases.

Animal Spirits and Demons

All of the world's religions attempted, in one way or another, to
answer the question of how human existence began. The people of
the Northwest Coast also asked themselves this question, but the
answers provided are surprisingly varied. Most of the cultures
recognized a being who created humans, the earth and the universe.
The creator did not, however, play a significant role in religious life
and was actually mentioned only in the creation myths.

Of greater significance to the Indians were the many supernatural
beings or minor deities, who appeared mainly in the form of animals.
Each culture had its own animal spirits and mythical figures. Only a
few were as widespread as Raven Yel, who played an important role
in the process of creation. Yel not only coaxed human beings out of
their shell, but placed the Sun, Moon, and stars in the sky, and created
islands and continents, mountains and valleys, rivers and lakes, fog
and rain—in short, the whole natural environment of his "playmates."
Human beings also owed the most significant aspects of their culture
to Raven Yel: fire, salmon and other foods, and knowledge about most
of their everyday material goods. But they also cursed him for causing
their mortality: When the creator went to the eagle to entrust him
with the job of awakening humans back to life after they had died, Yel
overheard him. As a carrion eater, he was displeased for he feared for

"Raven" (Raven with the Sun in his
beak). Silk-screen by Freda Diesing,
Haida.

his sustenance. He convinced the creator and the eagle not to bring people back to life, and since then, Yel has not had to worry about his well-being.

Raven Yel is not just the Prometheus of the Northwest Coast; his tricks and misdeeds provided the material for many amusing stories that make up the rich body of myths and legends of Northwest Coast cultures. Yel's heroic deeds and his mischievous tricks were told and retold from one generation to the next. In North American anthropology, this so-called "divine trickster" also appears in other forms and was known to the Plains Indians as Coyote, who is credited with the same or similar deeds as Raven Yel. It is unclear to what extent these stories influenced each other. The remarkable similarities do, however, indicate an extensive contact among cultures.

134

In 1980 the Nimkish Kwakiutl in Alert Bay opened the new U'mista Cultural Centre. Its front, decorated with a thunderbird and killer whale, is patterned after an old chief's house.

Page 135: This Lekwiltok Kwakiutl mask represents Bookwus, the wild forest monster. The animal-like ears are missing from the forehead. Confiscated in 1922, along with other potlatch goods, the mask was returned in 1979 to the new Kwakiutl museum in Quathiaski Cove, located on Quadra Island, British Columbia.

Another mythical animalistic creature with more than a regional significance is the thunderbird, which resembles an eagle and can swallow whales whole. It hurled lightning with its eyes, and its wings made the noise of thunder. Sun, Moon and echo were also known as personified beings along the entire coast and were formed in masks or other figurative representations.

There were countless other supernatural beings and demons on the regional and local level. The Haida believed that Wigit determined the longevity of human beings by pulling a stick out of a bundle on the occasion of a birth: The length of the stick determined what the expected length of the life of the newborn would be. The demons whom one could meet in the forest were rather sinister. The Kwakiutl feared Tsonoquoa, the giant woman of the woods, a cannibal who

gathered small children in a large basket, later to devour them. Kwakiutl children were quickly reduced to obedience when threatened with Tsonoquoa.

Often the animal spirits were a mixture of more than one animal, or they could transform themselves from one animal into another. The Nootka believed that a wolf could transform himself into a killer whale and vice versa, and there was the grizzly of the ocean, a creature half grizzly bear and half killer whale. The Tlingit, on the other hand, were not on good terms with the land otter people who bore a deep grudge against humans. They were probably justified, for the land otter was hunted to near extinction for its pelt. Otters revenged themselves by abducting people who were alone in the woods hunting or gathering berries. If the shamans could not save them in time, the abducted individuals were changed into land otters in order to replenish the otter population. The land otters were, therefore, not real animals, even though they appeared to be, but transformed humans. In the old times, that is, before the fur-trading period, the Tlingit did not hunt land otters.

Probably the most important and most widely known of animal spirits were the salmon spirits, also human beings in animal form. The salmon people commanded respect and were only approached with gratitude and reverence. To anger them could endanger the survival of the community, for the salmon people could decide to punish humans by sending few or no salmon to the coast and up the rivers the following year. Obviously, one had to be careful not to offend the salmon people. This required strict compliance with various procedures deemed to be essential to maintaining good relations. Because the Indians feared that the salmon people would not be treated respectfully by white people, who had no knowledge of the taboos and regulations, they did not want to sell salmon to the first white men.

The First Salmon Ceremony

The most important procedure was the observance and carrying out of the "first salmon ceremony." This ceremony was performed at the beginning of the fishing season each spring for each of the five species of salmon, as well as for other fish who swam up the rivers in large numbers, such as the eulachon. For some of the peoples the ceremony represented the beginning of the annual ritual "calendar," its high point taking place in the sacred wintertime. Franz Boas, the man who gathered the most extensive source material about Northwest Coast peoples, described such a ceremony for the coho salmon, only summarized here. The first four coho salmon of the season had to be caught individually with a hook and line. When the salmon bit, the fisherman encouraged him: "Hold fast salmon, hold fast!" Slowly he pulled the line in, and when the salmon was next to the canoe, he struck him to death with a single blow of a fish club. Then he prayed to the salmon: "Welcome, swimmer! I thank you be-

"Man with his Spirit." Silk-screen by Stan Greene, Coast Salish, in the style of a spinning whorl. In the original, the red color represents the physical and the white color, the spiritual existence of man.

A wooden shaman figure with human hair, earrings made of animal teeth and a leather apron. The figure, which represents a shaman singing and shaking rattles, is assumed to have been carved by a Tlingit shaman more than 100 years ago.

cause I am still alive and you have come back to our good place. Now, go home and tell your friends how you have arrived here and bring them all back, so that I may get some of your wealth, oh friend, oh Supernatural-One!" Each fisherman had his own version of this prayer.

Once on the shore, the fisherman's wife took the four coho salmon and spoke to the first of them: "Oh Supernatural-One, oh Swimmer! I thank you that you are willing to come to us to offer yourself as food. Let it be good, protect me and my husband, so that we may not die without cause." After this prayer of thanks she filleted the four salmon in such a way that the skeleton, head and tail remained as one piece. She threw the entrails into the water.

Meanwhile the fisherman had invited his numaym, his lineage, for the evening in order to ceremoniously eat the four salmon. This was absolutely necessary or the salmon would disappear forever. The guests were offered seats according to rank, and new eating mats were spread out before them. First they were served fresh water and then the most highly ranked guest spoke: "Oh supernatural friends! We are thankful that we see you still alive this year, as we also are still alive. Now we pray you to protect us, so that nothing evil will happen to us when we eat you. We know that only your bodies are dead, in order to provide us with sustenance, but your souls watch over us." With these words they ate the fish. After the meal, the fisherman again served water, while his wife gathered the remnants of the skeletons, bones and skin and left the house in order to throw them into the river. The life cycle of the salmon people would only repeat itself if all the skeletons and bones, as well as the entrails, were returned to the water. In other communities the first salmon was treated like a potlatch guest: It was seated in the place of honor and given gifts, and then eaten in the same ceremonial manner described above.

The Personal Guardian Spirits

Representations of animal spirits and the first salmon ceremony illustrate the extent to which religion and everyday life were inseparable. The latter was, moreover, determined by many taboos, proscriptions and regulations. Guardian spirits, usually in the form of animals, were there to help individuals achieve better mastery of their lives and to overcome the dangers of taboo transgressions. In some societies, a vision quest revealed the identity of the guardian spirit through fasting or castigation. In others, the guardian spirit was identical with the totem animal of the family, the lineage or a secret society, and it was passed to the individual through ritual. Such a guardian spirit created certain rights, for example, to become a great warrior, to participate in special ceremonies and to represent the spirit by wearing a mask in a ritual. In addition, some of these privileges had to be confirmed and legitimized by means of a potlatch.

One established contact with one's guardian spirit at least once a month by taking four baths a day, abstaining from sexual activity and eating only dried foods. This procedure cleansed the individual for contact with the guardian spirit, whose supernatural power was sought for success on the hunt, in battle and to heal a sickness.

The concept of animal spirits and personal guardian spirits in animal form indicates a relationship with nature that does not differentiate between animals and men. Animals and men are related to one another, can transform themselves from one into the other. Communication between men and animals was also possible, although it was usually only the shamans who had the capacity to understand animals. Who then were these healing specialists who were connected with the transcendental world?

Shamans

138

Our knowledge about the shamanism of the Northwest Coast has many gaps, due largely to the thorough teaching by the missionaries to the Indians. The missionaries saw the shamans not only as competitors, but also labeled them the instruments of the devil and disqualified them as healers. By the time of the first ethnographic studies were made toward the end of the 19th century, much of the knowledge about the powers of the shamans had been forgotten or was denied out of fear of reprisal, since all heathen practices had been forbidden. Further, specialized anthropological research into medical practices is a recent development. It is, therefore, particularly praiseworthy that several of the younger anthropologists have researched this area in scrupulous detail and have been able to provide us with a refined understanding of shamanism.

Both men and women were "called" to become shamans, often during a severe illness. Hallucinations, visions or frequent dreams were also signs of such a "calling," from which the individual could not escape. In fact, this prestigious social role was sought after, particularly if it was within the tradition of a family. A shaman might pass his powers on to a nephew who had been predestined for this role. The novice had to acquire the skills of a master during an apprenticeship that was often long. He had to become acquainted with and learn to control the spiritual helpers of the master. Their supernatural powers were responsible for his achievements. Close association with especially powerful healing spirits was not without its dangers; if the shaman's conduct was not correct, they could punish him by directing their power against him.

A new shaman was usually installed following the death of the teacher, and the ceremony was a public event. The successor was legitimized when he fell into a trance and made the same particular sounds and similar body movements as his predecessor. In this way, the spirit helpers identified themselves and announced that they accepted the successor. The spirit helpers could be land or water creatures, birds, insects, constellations of stars, natural forces such as wind and thunder or healing implements such as "soul catchers" (photo 69). Since there were powerful spirit helpers (and those of

The rattle of a Niska shaman from Gitlakdamix on the Nass River. Both sides are decorated with relief carvings. The reclining figure in the middle is surrounded by fur figures with spread arms and legs. (30 cm; NMM)

lesser significance), the shamans were ranged in a hierarchy of importance according to the identity of their spirit helpers. During the winters they often competed, showing off their abilities and, for entertainment, demonstrating sleight-of-hand tricks, such as swallowing knives, walking through fire and fighting with invisible evil shamans.

The shamans, who were both men and women, were held in respect and feared, since they were assumed to have the power to harm other people through black magic. In general, however, they served the village as clairvoyants, as in the story of Wideldal, and performed an important function as healers. Healing was closely related to concepts of what caused sickness in Northwest Coast cultures. Essentially, three types of illness were recognized: loss of

one's soul, the intrusion of foreign objects into the body of the sufferer and spirit disease. Loss of the soul was a serious illness that could only be cured by the most capable shamans. In a dramatic ceremony, the shaman entered into a trance and, summoning his powerful spirit helpers, embarked on a search for the lost soul. If he found it, he tried to convince the soul to return to the patient. Sometimes he had to free the soul from the sphere of influence of a malicious shaman. A spiteful shaman or spirit could also cause a disease-causing object to enter the body of his victim. The shaman treating the illness would remove this object from the body of the patient by, for instance, sucking it out and then destroying it. In the case of spirit disease, one sought the cause in ritual impurity or thought the patient to be possessed by an evil spirit. By means of a special healing ceremony, the shaman attempted to remove the contamination and cure the offense of violating a taboo, or he moved the spirit to leave the patient's body.

These healing ceremonies were public performances and brought the successful shaman much recognition. If the patient remained ill or even died, the shaman had to reimburse the family and had to deal with the ensuing hostility as well. If many of the shaman's patients died, the killing of the incompetent shaman with community approval was not unknown. The profession of shaman was frought with peril and only a few managed, thanks to their successes, to rise in the social hierarchy in the same way as successful warriors or artists. Among the Tlingit, a shaman could become chief or gain

Charm of a Chilkat Tlingit shaman. Made of bone, it is carved in the shape of a sea monster with its offspring underneath its belly and a cuttlefish behind it. (13 cm; SJM)

the respect of chiefs. For this reason, the Tlingit shamans were considered the most powerful on the entire Northwest Coast.

Where illness was determined to have been caused by evil influences; where powerful spirits made mischief; and where the hierarchical social order was by no means free of tension, it was necessary for there to be guilty parties. It is hardly surprising that suspicion and accusations of malevolence and magic were not rare occurrences. Women especially, but also children and slaves (although slaves were not actually considered to be people, but were thought of as possessions), were frequently accused of such misdeeds. Confessions were forced from them by torture, and the death sentence was the norm. Research in other parts of the world has shown that witchcraft and magic are common phenomena associated with

140

colonial conditions. To what extent this applies to the Northwest Coast remains an open question: there is simply too little information available from the time before contact with the Europeans.

The Sacred Winter

The sacred wintertime, which lasts from November until March and during which there is little seasonal work such as fishing and hunting, was the time when the spirit beings visited human beings and when all ceremonies took place. The social order was literally suspended; in place of lineage, clan and moiety, the secret societies made their appearance. Like the social order, they were organized hierarchically internally and in relation to one another, although only the noble classes were accepted into their ranks. These secret fraternities consisted of members with the same guardian spirit, and were further subdivided by age. A prospective member underwent an initiation rite, conducted by the father. Through fasting and mortification of the body—such as bathing in ice cold water—the novice was to experience a vision in which the guardian spirit of the particular secret society would appear to him. In this way, the noble classes were divided into the initiated and the uninitiated. The Kwakiutl had the most highly developed secret society system, which consisted of seven societies for men and three for women. The highest rank belonged to the hamatsa society, of which the highest-ranking numaym chiefs and the most influential shamans were members. Since cannibal beings appear in these dramatic ceremonies, it is also called the cannibal society, although it has been determined that cannibalism itself was not practiced in the pacific Northwest.

The wintertime was also the time during which mythical dreams were performed by the secret societies. Solo dancers and groups of dancers performed in their masks and, with the aid of diverse tricks, a number of special effects were achieved. Subterranean passageways and trapdoors made possible the sudden appearance and disappearance of dancers; hollow kelp stems used as microphones disguised voices; spirit pipes and horns produced ghostly sounds, and transformation masks impressed the puzzled audience. During the winter the chiefs and especially the shamans demonstrated their supernatural powers in order to affirm their rank, or at least to make a show of their powers. Only the members of the noble classes could participate in the ceremonies; here, as well as at the potlatches, commoners were tolerated only as spectators. The ceremonies also had no connection with economic activities. They did not represent a harvest festival or prayers for sustenance as in other cultures. After all, there was a surplus, if not for all, then at least for high-ranking families. On the other hand, the secret societies do not seem to have assumed just the role of leisure-time entertainers, but served to strengthen community cohesiveness. Presumably, the societies came into being during the early contact period when the fur trade engendered internal rivalries, which the societies with their integrating function sought to mitigate.

A hamatsa bird mask with movable beak. This monster raven serves Bakhbakwalanooksiwey, the cannibalistic creature of the north. Carved by Mungo Martin, one of the best-known artists and chiefs of the Fort Rupert Kwakiutl. (103 cm; MOA)

NOOTKA

On the west coast of Vancouver Island, from Cape Cook to about 40 km (24 miles) north of Victoria and on the northern tip of the Olympic Peninsula lives a group of people who are famous as whalers. Since the time of James Cook they have worn the name Nootka, which developed from an amusing misunderstanding. On March 29, 1778, James Cook reached Yuquot, the "friendly harbor," as he called it, with his two ships, the *Resolution* and the *Discovery.* (Today the Indian community at this site is still called Friendly Cove.) Cook anchored in order to take fresh water on board; furthermore, the ships were badly in need of overhauling. The local Mowachaht and their chief Maquinna, "the Stone," gave the English a friendly reception. Their first meeting was characterized by mutual respect. The Indians were impressed by the "swimming houses" of the white men, the British by the large population, for approximately 1,500 of the 6,000 Mowachaht lived at Yuquot. The misunderstanding arose when James Cook, who believed that the land where Yuquot was located was a peninsula, wanted to know the Indian name for the bay. The Indians thought he was asking where the arm of the inlet, which was visible toward the north end of the bay, led. In answer they made circular motions with their hands and repeated the word "notkak" several times. They tried to tell him that it was a matter of a narrow seaway which surrounded the island. "Notkak, in a circle," became Nootka, a name which not only applied to the bay, Nootka Sound, but also became a general term for the communities on the west coast of Vancouver Island. Today, like some of the other tribes of the Northwest Coast, the Nootka themselves have begun using a more traditional name, Nuu-chah-nulth, meaning "people along the islands."

James Cook does deserve credit for adopting Nootka Sound, the name he presumed the Indians to have given it. He had originally intended to name it King George Sound. The people themselves received a different name from Cook, one which has survived in the language still used by linguists. Cook wrote in his account: "If I had give them a name as a nation, I would call them Wak'ashians, after the word Wak'ash, which the women above all use frequently. It appears to express approval, agreement and friendship; for whenever they appear to be satisfied or very pleased, they call in unison "Wak'ash, Wak'ash."

There were further misunderstandings based on linguistic ignorance that marked the cultural contact between Cook's people and the Mowachaht. However, the time the English spent at Yuquot was apparently fruitful for both groups and, most important, it was friendly. The Mowachaht were interested in various trade goods, particularly all types of metal objects, whether knives or nails, and sometimes could not resist a little theft. Cook, however, was indulgent. The Indians had a clear idea of the comparative value of European goods and their own goods and could drive a hard bargain. When Cook's artist, John Webber, who accompanied the Cook expedition as documentarian, wanted to draw the interior of a Mowachaht chief's house (photo p. 176), the head of the household gave him permission only after Webber was prepared to pay with the shiny metal buttons on his elegant uniform. While he was working, the residents of the house repeatedly covered up the two carved house posts and only let Webber get a glimpse in exchange for another button. In this way, Webber lost practically all the buttons on his clothes and could barely keep his pants up. In the end, he left to posterity one of the most important ethnographic pictoral documents pertaining to Northwest Coast Indians in existence.

That which the Mowachaht offered the English was to have cataclysmic consequences for the Northwest Coast: the wonderfully soft sea otter furs (which confirmed the Russian reports of "soft gold"). After Cook departed at the end of April 1778, the life of the Nootka changed drastically as they were drawn into the conflict between the Spaniards and the English over who would gain primary rights to the west coast of America. In addition to this conflict, several native groups acquired European weapons and carried on wars among each other for primacy in the fur trade with the white people. The Mowachaht, Ahousaht and Clayoquot became the dominant powers. When a smallpox epidemic broke out in the middle of the 19th century, these small empires collapsed. Because of the density of their settlements, the original population of the Nootka is estimated to have been more than 30,000; in 1930 there were only 2,000 Nootka left. In the intervening years, the population figures have again risen. There are currently more than 4,500 Nootka in British Columbia and approximately 1,400 related Makah in the state of Washington. As of 1978 the Canadian Nootka have called themselves "Nuu-cha-nulth" (meaning All along the mountains) and they are hoping that the 200-year-old name Nootka, which was originally based on a mistake, will in time disappear from use.

75 The cleft, rocky coast, such as this area near the old Makah village of Ozette, located between Cape Alava and Sand Point, is not only picturesque and striking, but also dangerous to sea-going vessels. It is, therefore, hardly surprising that the Nootka had the reputation of being the most intrepid seamen in the Northwest.

76 The traditional and the contemporaneous: Are the totem pole and the television antennae the symbols of modern life for Indian people? The answer is probably "yes," reflecting the ambiguous attitude of the residents of this house toward their native culture. Many native people find it difficult to be proud of their history and tradition. For 100 years they have been told that their traditional way of life is uncivilized and to distance themselves from it as fast and as completely as possible. It is not easy to reconcile today's white world with the valuable cultural elements of the past.

77-80 Beginning on Vancouver Island as early as 1840, the timber industry has been British Columbia's most important economic base. Indians have worked in the lumber mills since 1856; in later years they also worked as lumberjacks and on log rafts. Today Indian people drive the massive lumber trucks (77) that deliver felled logs directly to the mills or they take them to the coast, from where the logs are floated to the pulp mills. Photograph 79 shows a log raft in Muchalat Inlet being moved toward the Gold River. The tug boat is steered by an Indian (78). The great lumber and pulp mill on the Gold River is close to the Mowachaht Nootka Reserve, which supplies most of the mill's employees. The mill produces cut lumber of every imaginable shape and size, as well as wood pulp, the mush substance basic to paper production. Most of the products are shipped out of the area. The thick smoke is indicative of the fact that environmental protection is not a serious concern. Air pollution and the clear-cutting of vast evergreen forests, with little attempt at reforestation, has led to protests by environmentalists. A precedence-setting case involves Meares Island, near Tofino on the west coast of Vancouver Island. An intense controversy has raged for several years over the preservation of that island's forests. The provincial government wants to turn the island over to large timber companies for clear-cutting, while environmentalists and the Clayoquot Nootka oppose such a move and want the island turned into a "tribal park."

81 The fishing harbor of Port Albion on Ucluelet Inland, where the Ucluelet Nootka have a small reserva-tion. Originally they also lived on Long Beach, which is now a part of Pacific Rim National Park.

82/83 Friendly Cove on Nootka Sound where James Cook once anchored and where the Swiss-English documentary artist, John Webber, captured the first images that the Europeans received of the Nootka. The Mowachaht Confederation made an annual migration to the Sound for a communal whale hunt. One of their communities was located at this site, which they called Yuquot, "where the four winds blow." Today Friendly Cove (the Yuquot Reserve) is inhabited by only a half-dozen people, Terry Williams, pictured, among them. Here she is wearing jewelry made with glass beads, a style that is actually typical of the Plains Indians.

84 This bear cub, which is probably sitting on the head of a larger bear, is a detail of a totem pole that was carved and raised around 1920. The totem pole stands in Friendly Cove. In 1929 a copy of it was presented to the then governor of Canada.

85 A small, densely woven basket with lid. The material is dyed and undyed sweet grass, interwoven to create a scene with water birds and a whaling canoe hunting a killer whale. The basket was acquired from the Makah in 1880. (24 cm; VM)

86 In carving this mask in 1985, the artist, Tim Paul, was inspired by a fairly rare motif in Nootka culture and was guided by the well-known original in the de Menil Collection in Houston, Texas. As the round, calling mouth indicates, this is a Tsonoquoa mask. The forest giantess was actually known only to the Kwakiutl, not to the Nootka. The northern Nootka, however, carried on commerce with the Nimkish Kwakiutl and also traded masks with them.

87 Long Beach, with drift wood. The beach, located halfway up the western coast of Vancouver Island, is part of Pacific Rim National Park.

▷ Thanks to the twined-weaving technique, this Nootka whale-hunting hat is waterproof. Jessie Webster (born 1909), a Nootka artist in Ahousat, located on Flores Island, wove this fine piece out of cedar bark fiber and dyed grasses. According to her account, this is a Maquinna hat, named after the powerful chief of the Mowachaht Nootka at the time of contact with James Cook. (26 cm; MOA)

77

78

84

85

COAST SALISH

The Coast Salish are the most heterogeneous of the Northwest Coast Indians; the only actual connection among them is that their languages belong within the same language family. The territory in which the numerous Salish peoples seek to survive on their small reservations is quite extensive. Their territory extends down both sides of the Georgia Straits as far as the Strait of Juan de Fuca and surrounds Puget Sound. The communities along the Fraser River as far north as the town of Hope are considered to be Salish as well. Those peoples living farther north are ethnographically classified as Inland Salish. Some of the Coast Salish groups, like the Pentlatch, have become extinct.

It is difficult to determine original population figures; the numbers vary from 15,000 to 20,000. The Coast Salish, too, suffered from warfare, particularly from attacks by the Kwakiutl and Nootka. However, diseases introduced by Europeans proved to be much more deadly. It is apparent from current demographic figures that the Coast Salish peoples have recovered. In British Columbia, 49 First Nations with a total membership of 12,200 are registered, and the Coast Salish in the state of Washington number more than 2,200.

In Salish territory, major cities such as Vancouver, Victoria and Seattle control the lives of Indians and non-Indians alike. The migration of Salish people to the cities is considerable. A large number of Coast Salish people live in the cities, where the chance of finding employment is far better than at the generally overpopulated reservations. Statistics show that only 15% of the Indians living in Vancouver are receiving welfare, as opposed to the national average of 70%. The level of education is also markedly higher, and an unusually large number of individuals belong to Indian organizations. It is no wonder that the Union of British Columbia Indian Chiefs is among the most influential in all of Canada.

The Niska Tsimshian played a significant role in the land rights controversy; the Coast Salish Sechelt also participated in the movement on behalf of Canadian native people for more autonomy and self-determination. The Sechelt was the first Indian nation to achieve legal recognition of a form of self-government developed by themselves. In so doing, they have provided a model for the First

Nations to achieve formal recognition of self-created governmental forms tailored to their needs. This is especially significant because of the lack of national support for Indian self-government by the federal or provincial governments. Examples such as those set by the Sechelt may have a more far-reaching effect than other political actions, because they educate Indians as well as non-Indians and, therefore, contribute to mutual understanding.

There is considerable work yet to be done in achieving this mutual understanding. Now, as in the past, there is widespread prejudice against Indian people. Many non-Indians notice the drunken Indians on city streets, who seem less concerned about publicly displaying their social problems than the average white person. And Indian people in the cities do have social problems, particularly if they are not sufficiently educated to gain employment. Being uprooted from their own community and isolated in city apartments contributes to their problems. Relationships and families may fall apart. The father may become an alcoholic, the mother may resort to prostitution, the children may run away and be removed from the parents by white social workers. The vicious circle continues.

For this reason the Indians in Vancouver, may of whom are Coast Salish, have established organizations to help their members survive in the urban environment. The Vancouver Indian Centre, for example, offers counseling for people of all ages, who may require vocational training, substance-abuse counseling, counseling for disfunctional families, or help with any number of issues. The center also provides legal advice and helps people negotiate the often difficult processes in obtaining welfare services. Adult education courses and a variety of recreational activities are also offered.

Indians often leave school before obtaining a degree and consequently do not have the prerequisites for career training. For the past 22 years, the Native Education Centre has offered people the chance to complete their high-school degree. Indians are also trained in those professions that qualify them for developmental positions within their own communities. No form of self-government can function without an educated and capable membership.

88 The most unusual and bizarre of all Northwest Coast Indian masks are the Sxwayxwey masks. The translation of the name is uncertain; it is supposed to mean "things which fly around in a circle," an appropriate description of the ritual in which the masks are worn. Among the Coast Salish, it is actually only the Halkomelem who have a Sxwayxwey ritual, a component of a potlatch. If a chief has suffered an insult, or when the status of the bride of a chief's son is to be elevated (for example, during a life crisis or a transition) a purification ritual is necessary. Two, four or more Sxwayxwey dancers appear in front of the house of the affected person and dance counterclockwise around a canoe filled with potlatch goods. They then approach the entrance to the house, from which steps the person in need of purification. He or she is led to the canoe by the dancers and seated in it. Up to this point, several women have been beating a steady rhythm on a large drum. They then begin to sing a song, and the dancers shake their shell rattles to the beat of the drum. The dancers approach the person in the canoe and brush cedar branches across his or her body. Four times the song and the purification ritual of the cedar are alternated. Finally the dancers retreat with dragging steps to the tent next to the house, where they had prepared themselves for the ritual. The mask pictured is of the snake-face type, identifiable by the two snake heads, which resemble horns, and the undulating lines which start at the neck and continue past the "stem eyes." The shape at the chin is thought to be a snake with front feet. This mask dates from the turn of the century and belonged to the Nanaimo Halkomelem. (51 cm; NMM)

89 Around 1900 this little basket was the property of the Thompson River Salish, an Inland Salish group who lived in the area where the Thompson flows into the Fraser River. They carried on an active trade with the Stalo Halkomelem, who lived further down the Fraser River, and so acquired this basket. A Stalo woman wove it out of cedar roots, dyed grasses and bark fibers. (16 cm; NMM)

90 The mats of the Coast Salish were originally woven of the spun woolly hair of the mountain goat and small dogs that were bred especially for this purpose. Although today weavers use sheep's wool, they have retained the traditional stylistic elements. The rug pictured was woven by Krista Point (see 112) who spun the wool herself and dyed it with natural dyes. She says that the pattern of connected triangles represents butterflies. (87 cm)

91 Evening on Howe Sound near Squamish, with Mount Ellesmere, elevation 1,768 meters (5,835 feet). The weather, so typical for the Northwest Coast, is foggy and cloudy.

92 Located between Vancouver and Squamish, Shannon Falls cascades 335 meters (1,105 feet) down into Howe Sound. It is one of the many beautiful sights on the Northwest Coast.

93 Two canoe-builders, members of the Stalo Halkomelem on the Chilliwack Reservation, doing the rough hewing on a pair of racing canoes. Each of the boats is fashioned from half of a split red cedar trunk and is intended to provide sufficient space for 11 men to paddle. In addition to the traditional adze, modern Indians also use axes and chain saws.

94 At the confluence of the Harrison and Fraser rivers, the Coqualeet'za (or Scowlitz), a subgroup of the Stalo Halkomelem, are fishing for sockeye salmon, which make their way to their spawning streams in July. They will catch 20 to 25 fish per hour with the net.

95 At a site nearby, the salmon is filleted in the traditional manner and hung up under a protective canopy to air dry. Shirley Norris uses modern steel knives for this work.

96 Portrait of the famous Coast Salish artist Simon Charlie (born 1919), who lives in Koksilah on Vancouver Island. Among his other works is a Sxwayxwey mask he carved for "The Legacy," the traveling exhibit of the Provincial Museum in Victoria.

97 The Coast Salish artist Susan A. Point created this modern round drum. It consists of a red cedar frame covered with deer skin. The thunderbird in double profile is painted in the style of a spinning whorl. This type of drum is used today in place of a drum board as accompaniment for the songs sung during a stick game (see 53). (44 cm)

▷ The Coast Salish are justifiably famous for their carved spinning whorls, as shown by the example above. The figure is surrounded by an otter on the left, a bird on the right, as well as by two bird heads positioned between the head and arms. The whorl is probably maple wood and was acquired in 1884 from the Cowichan Halkomelem on Vancouver Island. (21 cm; NMM)

89

161

90
91 ▷

What we don't like about the Government is their saying this: "We will give you this much land." How can they give it when it is our own? We cannot understand it. They have never bought it from us or our forefathers. They say now that they will give us so much land—our own land. These chiefs do not talk foolishly, they know the land is their own, our forefathers' for generations. Chiefs have had their own hunting grounds, their salmon streams, and places where they got their berries; it has always been so. It is not only during the last four or five years that we have seen the land; we have always seen and owned it; it is no new thing, it has been ours for generations. If we had only seen it for twenty years and claimed it as our own, it would have been foolish, but it has been ours for thousands of years.

THE FIRST NATIONS

It happened more than a hundred years ago. The new Canada, declared to be partially independent of Great Britain only 20 years earlier, exercised its power as guardian of the native people. On the basis of the Indian Act of 1876, the Canadian government distributed land in small parcels called reservations. The recipients of these generous gifts were the landowners themselves—a bitter irony of colonial history!

Little has changed since 1887, when David MacKay, a chief of the Lakalzap Niska, spoke the words quoted at the opening of this chapter to an investigating commission. One of his descendants, Roderick A. Robinson, Sr., a chief of the Gitlakdamix Niska, in a speech given in 1983 at the sixth conference of the Ecumenical Council of Churches in Vancouver, soberly observed that: "Our fight for justice began centuries ago, when a little boat with strange, bearded white men experienced difficulties at sea. With men who landed on an unfamiliar coast and arrogantly claimed ownership to the land. Our people, who had exercised control over 13,000 square km (5,200 square miles) of land since the beginning of memory, have always denied the incredible proposition that the simple act of discovery justifies possession of the land of those who are discovered. When it was our turn to 'be discovered' our fathers were surprised at this incredible arrogance." Less than 200 years have passed since the Niska Tsimshian and most of the other Northwest Coast peoples had their first experience with the "bearded discoverers."

The First Contacts

For a long time after the momentous voyage of the Genoese Christopher Columbus, sailing in the service of Spain, the Northwest Coast of America remained "untouched land." Which white man was the first to step ashore on this coast might be an important question to a European historian, but Indian people do not ask themselves such questions. They have always been there—ever since the creator provided them with this place. The Englishman, Francis Drake, is supposed to have reached the southern tip of Vancouver Island in

Petroglyph from Cape Mudge, located on Quadra Island. That the face represents a sacrificed slave is one of several theories about this and similar representations. This rock is now situated in front of the Kwakiutl Museum, Quathiaski Cove, B.C.

172

1579. Whether the Spaniards Lorenzo Ferrer Maldonado in 1588, Juan de Fuca in 1595 or Bartholemew de Fonte in 1640 sailed this far up the coast from Mexico is questionable. In any event, at that time the Spanish crown is unlikely to have laid claim to the coast north of Mexico. The other European powers only became interested in and started to quarrel over the New World in the 17th century, a time when they were interested in the Atlantic coast.

The Northwest Territory continued to enjoy its independence, although this would change drastically in the 18th century. It began with a country that previously had given no indication of interest in the New World, Russia. The enlightened modernizer of this empire, Peter the Great, was concerned with the contour of the coast in the distant Siberian north of the Chinese empire. He wondered whether a land connection to the American continent existed. The maps of the time showed only a large white area in the north of the Pacific.

Peter the Great's curiosity would not be satisfied during his lifetime. He died of pneumonia in 1725, shortly after commissioning the Danish sea captain, Vitus Bering, to make a discovery voyage. It was not until the summer of 1741, after one unsuccessful attempt, that Bering and the Russian Alexei Chirikov reached the southern coast of Alaska. Their respective ships were separated by fog and unfavorable winds. Chirikov sailed as far up as the 55th latitude into the coastal territory of the Tlingit. The first contacts were apparently of a hostile nature. Two boats, each manned by several men, made a landing; no one returned. Without risking further lives, Chirikov sailed back to Siberia.

Vitus Bering did not get much further. He found traces of a settlement on Kayak Island, but none of the residents. On July 16 the clouds lifted and he was able to see the St. Elias Mountains, whereupon he pressed for a return. Scurvy decimated his crew. His ship finally ran aground on the island named for him, not far from the east coast of Kamchatka. In December 1741 Vitus Bering died of the dreaded sailor's disease. Several of his men survived the winter and arrived home the following summer. They brought with them a number of fine sea otter furs, an event which would have far-reaching consequences for Indians of the Northwest Coast.

"Soft Gold"

The Russians had been carrying on a profitable fur trade with China for decades, but this commerce had begun to suffer as their wildlife became scarce. The voyages of Bering and Chirikov along the Siberian coast and to Alaska opened up new territories for the hunting and trapping of fur-bearing animals, of which the sea otter was among the most sought after. The fur of a fully grown sea otter measuring 1.5 meters (5 feet) and weighing 40 kilograms (88 pounds) brought a price in China which amounted to three years' income for one trapper.

The Czar left the exploitation of the newly discovered wealth in furs ("soft gold") to rough, ruthless, but hard-working trappers who were barely controled by the state. First the trappers subjugated the natives of the Aleut Islands. The trappers forced the natives to help them exploit the coastal waters from west to east until the fur animals were virtually extinct in that region.

Western Europeans learned of this wealth some 20 years later when Catherine II, empress of Russia, informed the western diplomats at her court of the fact. The Spanish were the first to react. They sent Juan Pérez Hernandez north from their Mexican base in San Blas. In 1774 he sighted the southern tip of the Alexander Archipelago and raised the Spanish flag at various sites, claiming the entire coast as part of Spain's territorial domain. Brief contacts were made with the Haida and Nootka (the motivation was apparently curiosity) without the Spaniards ever setting foot on land.

It was not long before the strongest colonial power on earth, Great Britain, sent its famous sea captain and explorer James Cook, a man already famous in his lifetime, on his third voyage to the South Sea with a special commission to sail along the Northwest Coast and through the Bering Strait in search of the Northwest Passage. Cook did not find such a passage, nor did he return from his voyage. He was killed in Hawaii during a disagreement with the natives there. His report of his trip along the Northwest Coast and his encounter with the Nootka, on whose coast he had spent a full month in 1778, created a sensation when it was published posthumously in London in 1784. Cook's account confirmed the Russian reports of a wealth of fur-bearing animals and the fabulous prices which were paid in China for

good quality furs.

Thereupon a race for the "soft gold" began. This product was to dominate world trade for more than 50 years. Beginning in 1783, the Russians built a series of trading posts starting from the north and working south. In this endeavor they found little hospitality with the Tlingit. This may have been due to the Russians' reputation as unscrupulous traders who did not pay well, or perhaps the Tlingit were merely maintaining their independence. In any event, in 1802 the Tlingit destroyed the Russian settlement at Old-Sitka, only three years old at the time, and one year later destroyed a second Russian outpost at Yakutat Bay. Under Alexander Baranov, the Russians were victorious in 1804, but they never completely subjugated the Tlingit. Relationships remained strained, particularly as the trappers and traders depended on the experience and help of the Indians.

Trade from 1774-1849

In contrast to other colonized territories, the trade situation was not entirely favorable to the whites. The Indians were tough and sometimes violent trading partners who were not gullible and fully understood the value of their own trade goods, particularly pelts and food. Because the Russians paid less, the Tlingit sometimes simply supplied them with less food. In 1812 the newly founded Russian-American Company was forced to build a settlement in northern California, Fort Ross, whose sole function was to produce food for the trading posts in Alaska. When the fur boom died down after 1830 and Fort Ross had to be abandoned in 1841, Alaska lost most of its commercial value to the Russians. In 1867, Alaska was sold to the United States for $7.2 million.

The true owners of Alaskan land, the Aleuts, Inuits and Indians, had as little to say about this transaction as their Indian neighbors in the adjacent coastal region of New Albion, when their territory became part of the British Empire. This happened in 1790, when the

Argillite pipe. Two sailors and two dogs are connected by an anchor chain. The hole for tobacco is located left of the middle. The wooden mouthpiece is inserted on the outside right. Such pipes were a typical mid-19th-century trade item. (42 cm; MOA)

Spaniards had retreated from the Northwest Coast. The natives barely noticed the change since the British had no need for the land in those early times. The main attraction held out by the Pacific Northwest Coast was the "soft gold," and to obtain it, the coast was visited by commercial shipping vessels of all nations, but most of all by American ships from Boston. Three decades were to pass before the English finally established their political supremacy. Between 1824 and 1849 they built a half dozen forts that served simultaneously as trading posts of the Hudson's Bay Company. As of 1821, this British company dominated trade in the entire Northwest, inclusive of the coastal regions in Russian Alaska, which they leased from 1839 until the sale of Alaska to the United States in 1867.

At the time of the earliest contact, the Native Americans were clearly astounded by the appearance of these bearded men in their "swimming houses." The "magic sticks" (guns) and the inexhaustible wealth of metal objects impressed them and led them to pay inflated prices for desirable trade goods. But they quickly learned that the white men were only humans like themselves. They soon recognized the value of their own products and demanded payment accordingly for what they traded: the foods, furs and art objects, which were increasingly desired by the traders. There were frequent conflicts, and many traders paid with their lives for misjudging their Indian trading partners. Many Indians acted as traders in their own right; the Tlingit, for instance, willingly made trips as far down as Puget Sound in their seaworthy canoes.

The first hundred years of the history of contact between white men and Native Americans on the Northwest Coast were characterized by an increasingly intense commerce between the sovereign Indian communities and white traders and fur companies. At first the Indians were mainly interested in metal weapons and tools, and later in sugar, rum, European clothing and blankets, tanned leather, sails and, not uncommonly, in slaves. The basic structure of their economic, social and cultural organization apparently changed very little. On the con-

176

trary, the hierarchical class system seems to have become stronger. The noble class wanted more artworks, such as ceremonial masks or totem poles, which could be more easily produced with the new metal tools. It follows that the reciprocal raids between Indian villages also increased.

Suppression and Resistance

In 1849 the English founded the colony of Vancouver Island and that year began the colonial suppression of the Northwest Coast Indians. In 14 treaties, entered into between 1850-54, the sovereignty of the Indians was still recognized and "unused land" was purchased in order to "assure friendly relations with the Indians," as one colonial official put it. These treaties were to be the last. Neither the second colony, British Columbia, created in 1858 (merged with the colony of Vancouver Island in 1866), nor the Canadian province of the same name, established in 1871, entered into treaties with the native peoples. It was the equivalent of denying Indian people recognition as sovereign nations. In 1865 they were given parcels of land as reservations, but the provincial government refused to recognize aboriginal land rights. This was hardly an unusual attitude in the last century toward the "heathen savages." It was assumed that Indians were, in any case, close to extinction.

While the Northwest Coast people experienced considerable cultural and economic growth during the fur-trading period, the second half of the 19th century was a time of extreme distress felt throughout the cultural fabric. The "Indian Commissioners" of the federal government's newly created Indian Department in Ottawa, as well as missionaries of every faith, influenced Indian culture enormously. They did away with warfare and slaves, and forbade polygamy, the potlatch, shamanism and the winter ceremonies. When necessary to enforce this "Indian policy," the Royal Canadian Mounted Police was called in, and many Indians became familiar with a hitherto unknown type of building—the jail.

It was not only the discriminatory politics of a colonial government bent on "civilizing" the natives that threatened the existence of Northwest Coast Indian cultures. A more serious disaster was the enormous death rate caused by European diseases which brought Indian peoples to near physical extinction. By 1862 measles, mumps, chicken pox, tuberculosis and venereal disease, as well as alcoholism and warfare between native groups, had severely decimated the population. Between 1862 and 1864 the entire Northwest Coast experienced a smallpox epidemic that killed more than a third of the Indian population. Unscrupulous traders helped spread the disease into the most isolated villages by selling the unsuspecting people infected blankets and clothing. The Kwakiutl, for example, were around 10,700 strong in 1835; in 1885 there were still approximately 3,000, and in 1925, they reached their lowest number with 1,854 members.

In spite of epidemics, sectarian missionaries, fanatic Indian com-

The interior of a chief's house on Nootka Sound, Vancouver Island. Watercolor by Johann Wäber, a documentary artist in the service of James Cook. The Swiss-English artist also went by the name of John Webber. (GA)

This noblewoman of the Nakoaktok Kwakiutl, identifiable by her shell nose ring and her gold bracelets, is wearing a cedar bark shawl and is painting a waterproof hat in the Haida style. Photograph by Edward S. Curtis, 1914. (GA)

A chief of the Babine Carriers, Athapaskan neighbors of the Gitksan Tsimshian, with whom they carried on an active trade, which explains why he is wearing a Chilkat blanket and a hat typical of Northwest Coast Indians. Oil portrait by Paul Kane, 1847. (ROM)

missioners and a not very gentle federal police force, the Northwest Coast Indians could not be subjugated. In contrast to other Indian tribes in North America, they had strong and efficient social organizations, which were an important factor in their unbroken resistance to total assimilation into Euro-Canadian society and culture. As mentioned, the forbidden winter ceremonies and the spectacular potlatches continued to be held in secret, even though valuable ceremonial items were confiscated and the participants could spend weeks and months in jail. The Indians fought as hard for their rights as workers in the growing fish industry as they did for their land rights and fishing grounds. In the 1880s Indian workers were already striking for higher wages and better working conditions. In 1919 the majority of the 9,000 workers, men and women who labored in the 97 canneries in British Columbia, were of Indian descent.

Borrowing from the Euro-Canadian tradition of political and labor organizing, the Indians in 1931 formed the Native Brotherhood of British Columbia (NBBC) to act as an umbrella organization for all Northwest Coast peoples. In 1936 the Kwakiutl founded the Pacific Coast Native Fishermen's Association, the actual labor union for Indian fishermen and cannery workers. After they joined forces with the NBBC in 1942, their main battle was over fishing rights, since their traditional fishing areas on the coast were being overfished by Russian and Japanese factory ships. The commercial Indian fishery is still threatened today by white sports fishermen and bureaucratic regulation by the provincial fisheries commission.

The Indian Act

Since 1876 the existential conflict between the Northwest Coast Indians and the white world that surrounds them has been part of the fight of all native people in Canada for self-determination. 1876 was the year a new law was passed by the parliament of the young Canadian state, the Indian Act, which gave legal weight to the de facto degradation of native people by reducing them to wards of the state. Those to whom the act applied were, of course, not invited to participate in the structuring of the law. Since then the Indian Act has been revised several times, the last extensive revision having taken place in 1951. Today the act still regulates the lives of Canada's registered Indians. On the one hand, it defines the special legal status of Indian people and helps preserve Indian identity. On the other hand, it prevents the Indian minority from achieving legal equality with the white majority and makes a self-determined life on the reservations a virtual impossibility.

The radical revision of this act has been a political necessity for native people for a long time. From the beginning, the Northwest Coast Indians have been attempting to do just this. In 1969 when the government of Prime Minister Pierre Trudeau proclaimed the total integration of the native people into the Canadian "melting pot," which would have been the equivalent of cultural ethnocide, the Northwest

Three generations of a Coast Salish family near New Westminster, capital of the colony of British Columbia from 1859-1868. Western clothes had found acceptance by the Indians. Photographed around 1887. (MM)

A Tsawatenok Kwakiutl girl with large haliotis earrings and a cedar bark shawl. Photography by Edward Curtis, 1914. (GA)

An old Koskimo Kwakiutl couple. Photograph by B.W. Lesson around 1912. (NMM)

Coast Indians were among the most visible opponents. In the summer of 1970 they founded the Union of British Columbia Indian Chiefs (UBCIC), which joined together with Indian organizations from other provinces to form the National Indian Brotherhood (NIB). The combined forces of all native people had diverse consequences. For instance, they were all recognized—Indians, Inuits and Metis (mixed blood)—in the new Canadian constitution of 1982, whereby their identity was finally given legal protection. The Indian Act has, in the meantime, been further amended to remove two offensive clauses. First, the discriminatory law that an Indian woman who married a non-Indian man lost her legal status as an Indian (although Indian men could marry whom they pleased without losing their legal identity as Indians) was repealed. Second, the native people regained

the right to determine themselves who qualifies for membership in their tribes or communities, a right which had been withdrawn with the 1876 Indian Act.

Self-Determination for the First Nations

These are the signs of a new political era, one in which the native people will have a place in the "cultural mosaic" of Canada. The conclusions to be drawn from this new attitude can only be the greatest possible autonomy and self-determination for Indian, Inuit and Metis people. For the native people, this goal is the logical extension of the legitimate right of all people to be self-determined, although this is a controversial concept in international law. Nonetheless, over the last

Gwayasdums, the main village of the Koeksotenok Kwakiutl on Gilford Island. Photographed in 1900. (PM)

several years the native people have been so bold as to designate themselves as the "First Nations." After all, they were the first on the American continent.

However the law with regard to native rights develops, the identity of the Indians is not dependent solely on their legal legitimacy. Another lesson which the Indians of the Northwest Coast have learned is that their cultural identity exists only if they live it. The lifting of various prohibitions when the Indian Act was revised in 1951 encouraged the revival of those cultural practices that had been suppressed. It also allowed others that had been practiced in secret to come into the open. The old ceremonies and even the potlatch are being practiced again as strong symbols of the culture of the Northwest Coast. These days such cultural practices emphasize com-

Chilkat dancers in the large theater in Haines, Alaska. Tlingits were not the only participants; young white people were allowed to join the group. Could this be genuine cultural exchange?

munity spirit; the ancient hierarchical class system has become obsolete. It no longer fits the concept Indian people have of themselves.

This new identity is not static. It is part of a process, another aspect of which is a new faith in themselves. In the course of the last hundred years, this self-reliance has been severely and intentionally undermined. It is, therefore, by no means an easy task for Indians to define their identity. So much has been lost or is preserved only in ethnographic records. For the coming generations, there will have to be a new bilingual and bicultural educational program so that today's children—tomorrow's adults—can be proud of their Indian heritage and capable of economic survival within Canadian society, an inescapable reality.

The foundations of a new self-determined Indian way of life have already been laid, but the reality of existing conditions, now as much as in the past, is appalling. A 1983 report to the Canadian Parliament showed that, compared to the national average:

— infant mortality among Indians is 60% higher
— only 20% of Indian children finish high school as compared to 76% nationwide
— the suicide rate is three times as high, with the majority of the suicides occurring in the 15 to 24 age group
— unemployment among Indians is 35% to 90%, depending on geographic area, compared to the national average, which tends to be around 10%.

These selected figures speak for themselves and are very similar to conditions prevalent throughout the Third World.

In order to effect long-term improvements in their living conditions, Indians—and not just Northwest Coast Indians—are demand-

ing that their traditional fishing rights be recognized and that an economically viable land base is assured for each community. It was the Niska who, in their 90-year-battle with the Canadian government, achieved a breakthrough that has raised legitimate hopes. A basically adverse federal court decision in January 1973 as to their rights to traditional Niska territory has, over the longer term, proven to be a positive development in Canadian law. Of the seven justices, six recognized the existence of aboriginal land rights, but three of the six were of the opinion that these rights were extinguished when the Dominion of Canada was established. Since the chief justice ruled against the Niska on procedural grounds, the decision resulted in a 4-to-3 split, with the majority ruling against the return of traditional lands to the Niska.

The federal government, nonetheless, was impressed that, for the first time in the legal history of Canada, a federal court had taken the existing land rights of the Native Americans seriously. They agreed to hear all claims to land, all complaints as to reparations due for treaty violations and all other claims for damages in order to achieve a final settlement. This has proven to be a lengthy and delicate process, since most of the claims involve existing economic interests. The large corporations oppose the payment of appropriate damages to native people for the taking of oil and mineral rights or the use of the forests and fishing grounds.

Indian tribes and communities could, however, benefit from a new national economic system to the same degree that a new, fairer world economic system would benefit Third World countries. It is hardly surprising that the Indians have joined with other under-privileged peoples worldwide in the international organizations in order to continue the fight for recognition of their rights in a global arena.

Indians want a new system in which it is possible once again to "be Indian" with dignity. They want to determine for themselves what their present and future should be like and what they need to do in order to survive as a small minority in a modern industrial society, without sacrificing their identity. Northwest Coast artists are showing very clearly that, not only have elements of their culture survived, but also that the culture is vital and in active ferment. Each one of these artists has discovered for her or himself just how painful and difficult the road to understanding one's bicultural identity as a "citizen plus"—as Canadian citizen and Indian—can be.

Physical education teacher and artist David Boxley of Metlakatla teaches an elective course on traditional Tsimshian culture. Far too often, knowledge of the old ways can be found only in books. People such as David Boxley are, therefore, more important than ever before to the student's identity development.

Pages 184/185: Shawtlans Passage, between Prince Rupert and Port Edward.

The greatest hope, as everywhere in the whole world, is with the younger generation. That these hopes are justified is illustrated by a true story told by the anthropologist Susan M. Kenyon in *The Kyuquot Way* (1980). In 1974 the then-chief of a Nootka community sold an old and famous Sun mask. His family and the entire village were shocked and saddened. A youthful member of the family stated his opinion about this sale: "He gave away his name. Now he is a nothing. The family is nothing. He threw it all away. He said that nobody cares about such things any more, but they do still care. They really do."

One day I asked my grandmother to let me see a special mask, which belonged to her husband, who was not home. I promised in exchange to carve a copy of the mask for her. Back then a feeling for and understanding of the art of wood carving was just developing and it had begun to control my carving knife. My grandmother refused to show me the mask, even when my mother asked on my behalf. My grandmother is a little old-fashioned and this mask was only used and shown to the people at a potlatch. After a while grandmother changed her mind and showed the mask to my mother, who asked her again to let me borrow the mask. Finally grandmother agreed, on the condition that I make two copies. After I had carved the two copies, I brought the original and one of the copies to grandmother and said: "Well, as you can see, it is really an exact copy."

THE VISIBLE HERITAGE

This reminiscence of the Nootka artist Tim Paul is quite revealing. His family had a mask which was concealed somewhere in the house of the owner and was only brought out and worn on the occasion of a potlatch. The mask must have been a masterpiece, for Tim Paul, a budding artist, to have had an interest in copying it. The mask did not exist purely as a work of art, however, but was primarily an object which lent power and prestige, a visible testimony of the social role and status of its owner on ceremonial occasions. If, for example, the mask represented the guardian spirit of its owner, exhibiting it outside of the specific ceremony in which this spirit plays a visible role would be tantamount to a lack of respect, and the owner could bring the fury of the guardian spirit upon himself. Tim Paul's grandmother still lived within this cultural tradition. Unfortunately, we do not know the end of the story, that is how she explained the handing out of the mask to its owner.

Ceremonial objects such as masks, rattles, Chilkat blankets and other items were publicly exhibited only on particular occasions. During the sacred wintertime they were taken out of the chests where they were stored to delight and sometimes frighten the spectators permitted to attend the ceremonies. The Kwakiutl had a particular love for imaginative, even farcical, masks with movable parts, such as the lower jaw, beaks and wings, which helped to heighten the theatricality of the ceremony. There were also the transformation masks: The outer form might be an animal mask, for instance, which would open up to reveal a second, inner mask, representing a human face. In this way the Indian concept that animals are humans in other forms could be visually illustrated.

All of these cult objects not only fulfilled their social and cultural functions within the framework of the winter ceremonies, but they also obviously grew out of the basic aesthetic needs of the Northwest Coast Indians. A talented artist, like a successful warrior, could gain great recognition, which often helped him achieve a high position within the community.

Drum in the form of a bentwood box. Its sides consist of a single board, notched and bent at the corners. Raven Yel is depicted in double profile with the Sun, which he placed in the heavens. Made in 1972 by Earl Muldoe, a Tsimshian artist in 'Ksan. (100 cm; NMM)

Totem Poles—The Crests of Chiefs

Totem poles have always been the most famous examples of Pacific Northwest Indian art. They could hardly be overlooked, even if we suppose that the first white men to reach the Northwest Coast did not find as large a number of totem poles as are in evidence on photographs taken at the end of the 19th century. The changes brought by the white men to the Northwest Coast are clearly visible in the wood-carving art of the Native Americans. First, the new iron tools made the work of carving the wood easier. Second, after warfare was outlawed, the continuing rivalries found a new avenue for expression in ostentatious displays of wealth intended to legitimize one's claim to social rank and power. Totem poles were the ideal vehicle for this: in order to outdo a rival, one erected a bigger and more beautiful totem pole.

It is likely that the oldest form of the totem pole was the house post, which supported the large roof beams. These carved posts are easily recognizable in the watercolor painting by John Webber, the artist from Bern who accompanied James Cook as documentarian on his third expedition (photo on p. 176). In many instances, it cannot be precisely determined what the carvings are meant to represent, although most often they are the crest animals or guardian spirits that indicate the social origins and rank of the owner. The support beams in the front of the house also served the function of exhibiting the family crest. One entered the house through a hole in the support beam for the ridgepole, an entrance so small and low that those entering had to bend down to fit through it. In time, high-ranking chiefs wanted larger crest poles, which then outgrew their support function and were placed decoratively in front of the house.

The most important type of pole was the memorial pole. It was generally commissioned by the high-ranking successor of a deceased person in order to confirm the legitimacy of his claims to the status and privileges of the deceased. The Haida carved so-called mortuary poles for high-ranking deceased persons; the coffin was supported on top of the pole. Another smaller type of totem pole was erected at graves as markers. Totem poles erected on the beaches served to welcome guests arriving by boat. The uses and significance of the poles varied from culture to culture, but they were more common in the north than in the south.

Among the carvings that might be found on a totem pole, first and foremost was the crest animal representing the lineage of the owner. Additional crest animals were added at the request of the owner, for example, those representing the moiety, or a mythical being which may have played an important role in the origin myth of the family of the deceased. As mentioned it is often fairly difficult to interpret the motifs on a totem pole in every detail. The analytical tools used to examine individual creations have only been available in the last 20 years. Gaining insights from such research is the work of Bill Holm, former curator of the Burke Museum in Seattle.

Two motifs by Tsimshian artist Roy Vickers: "salmon-trout-head ovoid" and "Tsimshian man."

Below right: Bentwood box with bear motif by David Boxley, Tsimshian. (88 cm, 1985)

Page 188: "Hole in the Ice." Totem pole of the wolf clan of the Gitksan Tsimshian in Kitwancool. Using ladders, one climbed through the hole into the house. On the pole appears, in addition to three wolves, a bear with his entrails visible. The figures around the hole recall an ancestor who saved his people from starvation.

Page 190: Four replicas of totem poles in Kitwancool: At far left is a totem pole of the frog clan with the ancestral mother and her frog children. The two poles to the right belong together and represent the wolf clan. The one to the left depicts Will-a-daugh with her wood worm children (see 42); after their death she changed herself into the mountain eagle Skim-sim.

Page 191: Heiltsuk transformation mask. Closed, it represents a hawk; open, the face reveals its human nature. (68 cm; NMM)

Nothing but Eyes . . .

The art work of the Northwest Coast Indians elicits amazement and admiration in many ways. If one studies a totem pole, one may recognize several animals at first glance. However, the stylistic elements can be confusing—is the bird really a raven or is it the mythological thunderbird?

Such questions can be answered only by carefully examining the structure of the design. First note the generally symmetrical plan; then observe that the artist has left no empty spaces, but has filled them with "eyes" (so-called ovoids) and other design elements. Exaggeration of size and expression, symbolism and abstraction are other stylistic elements. In two-dimensional representation, on Chilkat blankets, for example, symmetry was achieved by means of a split profile: The animal appears to have been split down the middle and laid open along its axis. It is difficult, if not impossible, to identify a figure when the animal's anatomical features—head, rump, legs, feet, ears, tail, etc.—are separated from each other and rearranged, apparently at random. Northwest Coast artists do not create a naturalistic design in their artwork. Instead, they paint or carve the animal or its body part in silhouette only. These "form lines" change constantly, becoming narrower, then wider, while color determines their importance within the design. The primary contoured lines are done in black, the secondary lines in red, and blue-green is used as a tertiary color. Not everyone used this color scheme; the blue-green tertiary color, for instance, was rarely used by the Haida. The most important universal element, however, is the contour or form line that circumscribes an area, not the area so circumscribed, which may be filled with random anatomical elements or with an "eye." This most characteristic design element appears in the varied curvilinear forms, ranging from perfectly round to egg-shaped, in double or triple lines or in the "salmon-trout's head" version. The term "joint eyes" is also

189

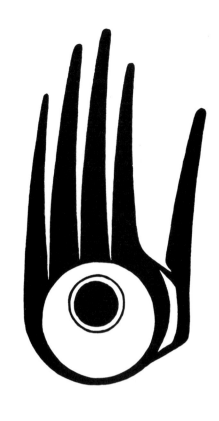

"Tsimshian hand" with an "eye" in the palm; a motif by Roy A. Vickers.

Below, a U-figure and bird claw with ovoid; motifs from Bill Holm's study of Northwest Coast art forms, 1965.

used, but often these are only space fillers. Eyelids and brows, U and S forms, feet and claws are also used as fillers and are rarely found in natural anatomical relationship to one another.

Few of these basic components help to identify the subject. More useful in this regard are a few characteristics typical of specific animals. The killer whale can be recognized by its striking dorsal fin; the beaver by its larger-than-life upper incisors and its crosshatched tail; the raven by its beak, which is only slightly bent to distinguish it from the strongly curved beak of an eagle. But eventually identification becomes more difficult, and the only solution is to reach for specialized catalogues or books. Experts are still debating diverse questions raised by Northwest Coast Indian art, among them, how this strikingly singular art form developed in the first place. One speculative theory suggests Pacific rim influences from East Asia, New Zealand and particularly Melanesia, where the art of wood carving was also highly developed. In opposition to this so-called diffusion theory, it has been shown that there is no evidence of a connection between these cultures. And so the respective cultural elements—in this case the art of wood carving—are independent "inventions." Even in the absence of answers to this and similar questions, anyone viewing the Northwest Coast carvings cannot fail to find them artistically fascinating.

Artwork for Trade

The artists of the Northwest Coast have always created usable art, whether for potlatches or other winter ceremonies, or for use as everyday items. Each work of art fit a specific cultural framework, even when it satisfied purely aesthetic desires. Through contact with white men, however, another art form developed which was intended for commercial purposes. It included the extraordinary stone carvings of the Haida, who began to develop these items around 1820 with the intent of trading them for European goods. Near the community of Skidegate on Graham Island are a number of argillite deposits, a stone with a degree of hardness somewhere between slate and alumina. Its carbon content imparts the typical black color. The stone is related to the red, iron-rich catlinite, used by Plains Indians to carve pipes. The Haida's argillite deposits provided an especially pure stone, well suited to carving. The quarry, encompassing approximately 45 acres, has been classified since 1941 as reservation land and is under the sole jurisdiction of the Indian community at Skidegate.

In its natural environment the stone is relatively wet. After removal from the quarry, it must be dried slowly to prevent cracking while it is being worked on. The restoration of old pieces has shown that the water content of the stone has little effect on its hardness. The introduction of metal-carving tools must have benefited the stone-carving art, which was originally restricted to the Haida. This historic fact also applies to wood carving, which reached both a qualitative and quantitative peak in the 19th century, following the introduction of metal tools.

The Haida first produced argillite pipes, which were very popular with the white men. In terms of decorative style, they utilized traditional patterns and motifs, always remembering the rule that certain motifs were the property of particular persons and were not generally available. The limiting effects of this law, along with other factors, led to greater utilization of Euro-American motifs. In addition to pipes, later carvings included platters and similar items. Toward the end of the last century, scientific interest in Northwest Coast culture increased noticeably and, due partly to commissions from museum curators and private collectors, Haida artists again began to produce more traditional items, such as miniature totem poles.

Haida argillite platter made in the 1880s, showing two killer whales. The rim is inlaid with opercula, sea snail "plugs." (42 cm; MOA)

Since the 1960s native art on the Northwest Coast has flourished again. Artists are now utilizing modern techniques, such as silkscreening; new marketable items such as jewelry crafted in silver and gold are enriching traditional art forms. The artwork of the Northwest Coast Indians has become increasingly visible and is fully recognized as part of world art. An American museum curator speculated a few years ago that the most beautiful pieces were still concealed in the chests of individual families who treasure their traditions, in order to hide them from the "profane eyes of the white man." Artists like Tim Paul, however, provide us with the opportunity at least to admire copies of these treasures.

98   In 1976, on the occasion of the Bicentennial celebration in the United States, the artist Duane Pasco of Seattle won a competition in Sitka that resulted in a commission to create a "Bicentennial totem pole." This totem pole now stands in front of the Visitors' Center in Sitka National Historical Park. The base figure holding the halibut hook and the rattle represents the Northwest Coast Indian, who had a rich material culture and a magnificent ceremonial life before the arrival of white men.

99   Next to his house in Metlakatla, David Boxley has turned a shed into a workshop, where he spends his spare time working on his art. At the time we visited him in 1985 he was carving a crest board with the heraldic animal of his family, an eagle represented in double profile.

100   In his large studio next to Saxman Totem Park in Ketchikan, Nathan P. Jackson works on a new totem pole for a ceremonial house planned for the community. As with all Northwest Coast artists, his most important tool is the adze.

101   On the Northwest Coast, artistic skills are often learned from a recognized artist. An apprentice works with the master on the same piece, for example, on the symmetrical opposite side of a totem pole. In the summer of 1985, Nathan P. Jackson instructed two apprentices simultaneously, Israel Shotridge, left, and David Jensen, right.

102   Like many other Haida artists, Garner Moody, born in 1958, specializes in argillite carving. Among his teachers are his uncle, Rufus Moody, and Alfred Collinson. Garner Moody lives in Skidegate.

103   The Tsimshian artist Ken Mowatt is known for his rather modern silk-screens. Here, in his studio in Hazelton, he works on a new silk-screen.

104   Reggie B. Peterson was employed in 1985 as wood carver and silversmith at the Southeast Alaska Cultural Center in Sitka. Here the Tlingit artist puts the finishing touches on an alder wood mask.

105   On this silk-screen created in 1985 in the traditional style—if that can even be said about this new art form, which is relatively new to Northwest Coast art— Tony Hunt has drawn three important heraldic animals. At the top is the eagle, his claws on the head of a killer whale, which is resting on a beaver.

106   In her home in Ketchikan, Holly Churchill-Burns demonstrates the art of weaving a Haida hat from spruce roots. When she was a child, she says that she often had to help her mother, Delores Churchill-Peratrovich, gather roots and cedar bark, and that she made early attempts at basket-weaving. At that time she was a less enthusiastic weaver than her sister, April Churchill-Varnell. Now, however, she has begun to feel that she, too, wants to continue this tradition of her Haida family. She was inspired, in part, by an exhibition of contemporary basket-weaving in Alaska dedicated to her grandmother, Selina Peratrovich, a Haida woman from Masset.

107   In the summer of 1985 the Indian Cultural Center in Sitak hired Margaret Gross as sewing instructor. The art includes the creation of so-called octopus bags and button blankets (see 29), two Tlingit specialties.

108   Richard Hunt, master carver at Thunderbird Park, part of the British Columbia Provincial Museum in Victoria, paints a Gakhula mask. The Gakhula beings appear in the Klasila dance ceremonies that were performed in the winter. They mockingly interrupted the dance procession and were then escorted from the ceremonial house.

109   Susan A. Point, the best-known contemporary Coast Salish female artist, engraves a silver bracelet, precision work that requires steady hands. The work platform can be moved in any direction.

110   This silver bracelet, depicting Raven Yel with the Sun, is attributed to an anonymous Tsimshian artist. (5 cm; MOA)

111   In 1972 Bill Reid created this silver killer whale on an argillite stand, copying his own 1970 masterpiece, which he had worked in gold for the traveling exhibit "The Legacy." The shape was created by means of the "lost-wax" method. (6 cm; NMM)

112   Krista Point, Susan Point's niece, is considered an excellent weaver of typically Coast Salish rugs. The loom is an improved version of the simpler looms used in earlier times (see photo on p. 48).

▷   "Salmon": a crest board with a salmon carved in relief with a superimposed fish mouth, by David Boxley of Metlakatla. (76 cm; 1985)

98

101

102

103

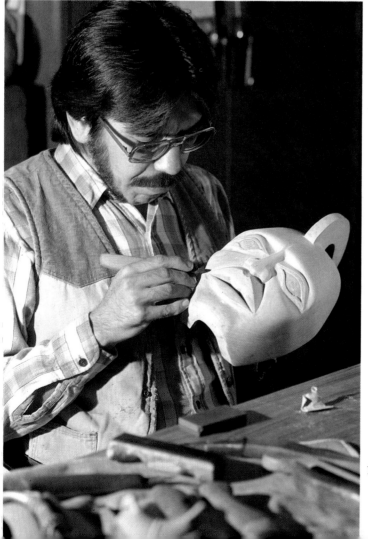

104

105

PORTRAITS OF THE ARTISTS

Little information is available about the artists of the past. All we know is that there were some professional artists who did contract work for which they were paid. In the case of a large project, such as a totem pole, the artist and his family would move into the house of the person commissioning the work until it was completed. It was not the practice of the artists to sign their works, which is why the creators of only a few old pieces can be identified. Not until the end of the last century did artists begin to identify their own work.

Since the 1950s an increasing number of anthropologists and museum curators have become interested in the art of the Northwest Coast Indians and have helped save the old artwork from decay by conserving, restoring or replacing totem poles with replicas. This has encouraged Indian artists, such as the Haida artist Bill Reid, to develop their art into a profession and to teach younger artists. This is how the Northwest Coast Indian Art School came to be founded in 'Ksan, near Hazelton, British Columbia. The school has become a mecca for artists from the entire Northwest Coast.

In all of the following biographies of artists, it is clear that they studied the art of Northwest Coast people in general before they concentrated on their own cultural heritage as, for example, Tlingit or Coast Salish. For lack of continuity in passing this information from generation to generation, the artists often have to acquire the traditional styles of their own people by studying museum pieces. This is especially true of the Nootka and the Coast Salish.

The choice of the 11 artists who are portrayed in alphabetical order on the following pages, each with a short biographical sketch and an example of a recent work, is largely coincidental. We did take care, however, to assure that each major cultural group would be represented and, in addition to several well-known artists, have included younger representatives of Northwest Coast art who are not as widely known.

"Woman mask with lip plug and tattoos." Bill Reid, Haida. (22 cm; MOA)

Born in 1952 in Ketchikan, David Boxley grew up with his grand-parents in the Tsimshian community on the Metlakatla Reservation in Alaska. After high school he attended Seattle Pacific University where he received a teaching degree. Several years ago he returned to Met-lakatla with his wife and two children. He teaches health, physical education and, most recently, Indian history.

His grandfather introduced him to the tradition of the Tsimshian and he has been fascinated with the culture ever since. It was only after finishing college, however, that he started to come to grips artistically with his Indian heritage. In 1975 he painted a series of 50 oil paintings titled "How They Lived," which depict his ancestors in their daily and ceremonial life.

Since 1979 David Boxley has been developing special mastery in the art of wood carving. Completely in the service of Tsimshian mythology, he carves totem poles, canoes, rattles, combs and wooden storage boxes (bentwood) in the traditional style. He also creates silk-screen prints, as do nearly all of the Northwest Coast artists. The growing number of his commissions and exhibits bear witness to the recognition his work is receiving. In Metlakatla he is recognized as one of the initiators and supporters of Indian self-awareness. In honor of his grandfather, he carved a totem pole which he had ceremonially raised on the occasion of a potlatch in 1982, the first held in Metlakatla in 95 years.

"Four Clans United": wolf, raven, eagle and killer whale. Silk-screen in the style of a painting in a drum. (31 cm; o.J.)

Freda Diesing, born in 1925, is the oldest artist in our selection, although she did not, in fact, begin wood carvings until she was 42 years old. Without any training, she carved a small display with canoes and dolls for the 1967 Indian Festival in Prince Rupert. A year later she entered the newly founded art school in 'Ksan near Hazelton. There she received expert instruction in wood carving and silk-screen techniques from such well-known teachers as Bill Holm, Robert Davidson and others.

Freda Diesing is the daughter of a Haida family from Masset, on the Queen Charlotte Islands. She has, however, always lived on the mainland, first in Prince Rupert, and now in Terrance, British Columbia. She specializes in masks and bowls made of alder wood and has carved one totem pole to date, which stands in Prince Rupert, the town where she was born. Her first major success came in 1971, when one of her masks was shown in a significant art exhibit in the British Columbia Provincial Museum in Victoria, an exhibition appropriately titled "The Legacy." This exhibit was so well received that it went on the road in 1975. It was shown in several other Canadian cities and finished its tour as the opening exhibit of the new City Art Centre in Edinburgh, Scotland, in 1980.

A part of Freda Diesing's income comes from the sale of art print greeting cards, a considerable success. Today Freda Diesing is also an instructor. She teaches largely in Prince Rupert, and several of her students, among them Dempsey Bob, Gerry Marks and Norman Tait, are already beginning to make names for themselves.

"Scana with the Woman" (Killer Whale and Woman). Silk-screen (1980).

209

Stan Greene was 22 in the summer of 1975 when he started as a student at the art institute at 'Ksan. He was immediately greeted with prejudice based on a false assumption. He remembers that when he first met the instructors and the other students, the northern artists were amused that he wanted to learn wood carving. They laughed and told him that the Coast Salish could not carve.

This point of view was not surprising. Until just a few years ago, the wood carvings of the Coast Salish were largely ignored. Traditionally, these works of art were not traded but remained the personal property of individuals or families. Consequently, other Northwest Coast peoples had little exposure to them. In addition, the Coast Salish came under the strong influence of white men earlier, which brought the development of their art to a virtual standstill.

Widely known, however, are the Sxwayxwey masks, which seem so foreign to our eyes, and the spindle whorl which, in pre-Columbian times was often carved from soapstone. Inspired by these spindle whorls, Stan Greene painted their motifs in watercolor, and reproduced them through silk-screening. Silk-screens have since become his specialty.

In contrast to traditional examples, such as wooden statues that have a naturalistic style, Stan Greene has developed his own style, which is unmistakably Salish. He and Susan A. Point are among the few Coast Salish artists who are reviving the legacy of their forefathers after decades of neglect. Stan Greene lives with his wife, three daughters and a son in Chilliwack, located in the Fraser Valley east of Vancouver.

"The Eagle and the Salmon." Silk-screen in the form of a spindle whorl carving. The faces symbolizes the human essence of the animals. (o.J.)

RICHARD HUNT   KWAKIUTL

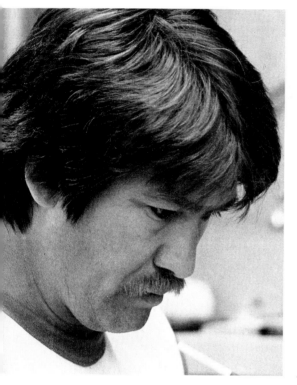

Born in 1951, this artist began to carve in wood at the early age of 13, under the direction of his father. While he was still in junior high school in Victoria, he utilized his spare time to develop the basis for his career as an artist. After completing his schooling, he perfected his craftsmanship in the studio of his brother, Tony Hunt. He soon began to receive commissions from the British Columbia Provincial Museum and, in 1974, followed in his father's footsteps to become master carver of Thunderbird Park, the open-air museum of the Provincial Museum.

In recent years he has carved numerous replicas of old pieces for the Provincial Museum, mainly masks and totem poles, but he has also created many new works. A large part of his work can be viewed in the fascinating permanent exhibit of the museum called the "First People's Gallery." Many of his pieces were also part of "The Legacy," a traveling exhibition, with which he was extensively involved and which he accompanied from one museum to the other.

His work not only takes him all over the province, but also out of the country to Chicago and London, where he has demonstrated his craftsmanship and sometimes performed as a dancer. Together with Tim Paul, for example, he carved an 8-meter (26-foot) totem pole for the Captain Cook Museum in Middlesbrough, England. It was raised in a 1979 ceremony honoring the 200th anniversary of the English explorer's death.

Richard Hunt was specially honored when one of his masks was presented to Queen Elizabeth as a gift during a state visit to Canada in 1983.

"Kwa-Gulth Moon" (Kwakiutl Moon). Silk-screen print with U and S forms, as well as the color yellow, typical characteristics of the Kwakiutl style. (65 cm; 1978)

214

Probably the best known of contemporary Kwakiutl artists is Tony Hunt, who was born in 1942 in Alert Bay and spent his early years in Fort Rupert. His family has lived in Victoria since 1952. He learned the art of wood carving and ceremonial dance from his famous grandfather, Mungo Martin. After his grandfather's death in 1962, Tony became assistant to his father, Henry Hunt. In 1970 Tony Hunt opened the "Arts of the Raven Gallery" for the express purpose of offering qualitatively better craftsmanship than was then available in the souvenir shops. For the past 17 years, since leaving his position with the museum, he has dedicated himself exclusively to promoting Northwest Coast art. Several artists who now produce works commissioned by the gallery were instructed in his gallery studio.

Tony Hunt carved a large number of totem poles which are on exhibit around the world, from Sydney to Montreal, from Buenos Aires to Osaka. His artworks have been shown in more than two dozen exhibits and his versatile talent has been recorded in more than 15 documentary and video films. He has received a variety of honors for his efforts on behalf of Northwest Coast art.

Tony Hunt has not only remained true to his origins as carver of totem poles, but he has also helped to revive the old ceremonial traditions, such as the dances, in which he actively participates, or potlatches in their new form. In honor of Mungo Martin, he and his father, Henry Hunt, carved a memorial pole that is more than 10 meters (33 feet) high and raised it in 1970 in the old cemetery in Alert Bay.

"Raven." Symbol of the "Arts of the Raven" gallery in Victoria. Tony Hunt explains a halibut motif on a new totem pole for his Fort Rupert Kwakiutl community.

NATHAN P. JACKSON   TLINGIT

We met Nathan Jackson in a large shed where he and two apprentices were carving a totem pole. He was wearing overalls and a wool cap, and only his age gave us a hint as to which of the three was the best-known Tlingit artist in southwest Alaska. He was born a member of the salmon clan near Haines, a clan that belongs to the raven moiety within the Chilkoot tribe. The old traditions, which have had a lasting effect on the artist, were passed on to him by his uncle and grand-father.

After serving in the military, he enrolled in the Institute of American Indian Arts in Santa Fe, New Mexico. From 1962 to 1964 he studied graphics, design and silk-screening there. He then returned to Alaska and, in 1967, became in independent artist. Nathan Jackson usually works under contract, and the more time passes, the less he can complain about a shortage of commissions. His works—totem poles, house fronts, bentwood boxes and masks—are on exhibit in Seattle, Salt Lake City, Chicago, New York, Boston, London and Kobe. His work is most visible, however, in Alaska, from Ketchikan to Fairbanks. To name just a few examples: An eagle relief welcomes visitors to the airport in Ketchikan; two 12-meter-high (40-foot) totem poles stand in front of the Centennial Building in Juneau; and the Sitka National Historical Park has several totem poles that have either been restored or reproduced by him.

Nathan Jackson has had numerous opportunities to exhibit and demonstrate his craft, for example, at the 1964 World's Fair in New York and in Washington, D.C., at the Smithsonian Institution's Folk Festival, where he also participated as a Chilkat dancer. In addition to his studio work, he is an art instructor at the Community College in Ketchikan, where he has lived with his wife and two children since 1972.

"The White Man in the Land of the Wuckitan Tlingit." Detail of a totem pole in front of Centennial Hall, created in 1981 for Juneau's Centennial celebration.

KEN MOWATT TSIMSHIAN

In the small community of Kitanmax between the Skeena and Buckley Rivers, the Gitksan artist Ken Mowatt was born in 1944. He still lives there with his wife Jane. Like many of his generation, he was raised by his grandparents who, by means of stories, myths and legends, tried to give him an inkling of the traditional life style of their people. At first this had no recognizable effect on him, but the art school in the neighboring open-air museum at 'Ksan beckoned in 1969. It is here that he learned his craft.

At 'Ksan, Ken Mowatt came to appreciate the importance of working together with other artists as he cultivated an active exchange of experience with Vernon Stephens, Earl Muldoe and Walter Harris. Above all, he was interested not only in learning the art of his ancestors, but also in developing it further, to make his own contribution to traditional Tsimshian art.

More than any other medium, wood carving became a passion for Ken Mowatt. His sensitivity to form and figures has made him one of the most expressive artists of the Northwest Coast. Proof are the numerous totem poles, masks, bowls and wooden shields, as well as his silk-screen prints, which are enjoying greater recognition and dissemination. Ken Mowatt also occasionally offers courses at the Northwest Coast Indian Art School at 'Ksan.

"Loon." Silk-screen. (39 cm; 1985)

TIM PAUL

Tim Paul was born in 1950 in the small lumberjack community of Zeballos on the west coast of Vancouver Island. His father belonged to the Hesquiat and his mother to the Ehatisat group, which are part of the larger group of people called Nuu-chah-nulth, generally known as Nootka. Because his father moved the family frequently in his search for work, Tim Paul spent the first years of his life largely in isolated fishing and lumbering villages.

He spent the better part of his school years in boarding schools run by Catholic priests, monks and nuns. The repressive atmosphere there was discouraging: Indian native languages and traditions were considered heathen and barbarian, and the children were treated accordingly. For Tim Paul, this time in his life was a torment. His only happy memories are the summer vacations spent at home with his parents or grandparents. He was glad to be able to finish his schooling in Victoria, where he could live with his older sister.

After school he pursued job as a lumberjack and laborer in a sawmill, then worked at the Victoria Native Friendship Centre until he began his career as an artist in 1974. He was fortunate to be able to work at the British Columbia Provincial Museum from the start, first as apprentice to John Livingston and Gene Brabant, later together with Richard Hunt. After he had had an opportunity to work in virtually all Northwest Coast styles, he gained special expertise in the traditional styles of his own people by utilizing the museum's collection. Today Tim Paul is recognized as a pioneer in the revival of Nootka art. Due to his status as a museum artist with a regular income, it is possible for him to continue to develop a process, which is clearly recognizable in his works, ranging from totem poles, masks and rattles to silk-screens.

"Hesquiat Hunter" (A Hesquiat-Nootka hunting a killer whale). Silk-screen. (O.J.)

REGGIE B. PETERSON   TLINGIT

We met Reggie Peterson on a rainy autumn day in the studio of the Southeast Alaska Indian Cultural Center, which forms part of the Visitor Center of the Sitka National Historical Park and is run by the Alaska Native Brotherhood. Peterson has a permanent position here as wood carver and silversmith.

Reggie Peterson was born in 1948 in Juneau, today the capitol of the state of Alaska. After completing school, he attended the American Academy of Art in Chicago for four years, acquiring the basic skills for his career as an artist. He has lived in Sitka since 1977, where he studied with master carver and silversmith Edwin Kasko for two years.

As of 1979 Reggie Peterson has not only been resident artist, but also teaches young art students and acts as a visitor's guide in the museum of the Visitor Center and the park, where the Kiks•adi clan once defended their fortified village against the Russians led by Baron Baranov. Reggie Peterson feels very close to the history and culture of his people. He has offered cultural history courses about the Tlingit for the elderly and is frequently an instructor at Sheldon Jackson College, where he teaches woodcarving and a general course on Northwest Coast art.

Among his best known works are the reproductions of four house posts and a wolf totem pole, the originals of which were in a Kaigani-Haida settlement, the now abandoned community of Old Kasaan. Around the turn of the century, Saanaheit, who was then chief of the village, gave the posts and totem pole to the governor of Alaska, and they eventually found their way to the Historical Park in Sitka.

In the studio of the Cultural Center, Reggie Peterson mainly creates works that are intended either for museums or are privately commissioned. He has had a private contractor's license since 1983 that allows him to independently accept and seek out commissions. His work is receiving increasing recognition, although he is most well known in southeast Alaska.

Shark mask made of alder, with hair and haliotis inserts. The artist carved it to qualify as a master carver in 1980. It represents the crest of his clan.

SUSAN A. POINT   COAST SALISH

The artist Susan Point is a member of the Musqueam community, whose reservation is located on the north tributary of the Fraser River in Vancouver. While in school she occasionally spent time drawing and painting, but did not become seriously interested in art until she was 29, when she took a course in silver jewelry making while on a maternity leave. The four-week course offered by Vancouver Community College instantly inspired Susan Point to try to be a silversmith. She has such extraordinary talent that her success was immediate. It was still during this same year that she tried her hand at working with gold. Her bracelets, pins, rings and earrings were an instantaneous success. Later that year, she took a course in silkscreening, an art in which she also acquired considerable skill.

Like many other Northwest Coast artists, she worked in all of the styles of the coastal peoples before she concentrated on her Coast Salish identity. Anthropologist Michael Kew at the University of British Columbia, himself married to a Coast Salish woman, encouraged Susan Point to find her own style and provided her with much useful information and slides about the traditional art of her people.

Today Susan Point (who from 1981 until 1985 was known by her married name, Susan Sparrow) is recognized as one of the most striking Coast Salish artists. Her love for simplicity and precision is her strength, and it is not surprising that her work can be found all over the world—in Japan, Australia, Germany, Switzerland, Great Britain, the United States and Canada.

''Two-Headed Serpent.'' Silk-screen based on a carved motif found on the handles of combs. (35 cm; March 1983)

ROY H. VICKERS   TSIMSHIAN

Although he was born in the Niska village of Greenville in 1945, Roy Vickers spent his childhood years in Kitkatla and Hazelton, where he also attended elementary school. He later completed his schooling in Victoria. It was during that time that he developed a great interest in his Indian heritage.

He was creating silk-screens when he was only 19, and became one of the first Indian artists to use this modern technique. Vickers also taught himself wood carving. He was so talented as a carver that he was able to attend the Northwest Coast Indian School at 'Ksan, where he completed his degree in 1974.

For the past several years, Roy Vickers has lived in Tofino, on Vancouver Island's west coast. His multifaceted work takes him all over British Columbia, however, since he occasionally shares his artistic skills in public courses. In addition to television appearances, he worked with a Vancouver ballet troupe that had been inspired by his silk-screen "Creation of Eve" to produce a ballet with the same title. Vickers designed the costumes.

His work—wood sculptures and serigraphs, or silk-screens—have an international audience and can be seen in many museums and private collections.

"Steelhead." Silk-screen. (46 cm; o.J.)

BIBLIOGRAPHY

228

Arima, Eugene Y.: The West Coast People. The Nootka of Vancouver Island and Cape Flattery, B.C. Provincial Museum, Victoria 1983

Berger, Thomas R.: Village Journey. The Report of the Alaska Native Review Commission. Hill and Wang, New York 1985

Blackman, Margaret B.: During My Time. Florence Edenshaw Davidson, A Haida Woman. Douglas & McIntyre, Vancouver 1982; University of Washington Press, Seattle 1982

Boas, Franz: Kwakiutl Ethnography. Edited by Helen Codere. University of Chicago Press, Chicago 1966

Chevigny, Hector: Russian America. The Great Alaskan Venture 1741-1867. Binford & Mort, Portland 1965/79

Codere, Helen: Kwakiutl, in: E.H. Spicer (Hg.), Perspectives in American Indian Culture Change. University of Chicago Press, Chicago 1961/69

Drucker, Philip: Cultures of the North Pacific Coast. Harper & Row, New York 1965

Duff, Wilson (Hg.): Histories, Territories, and Laws of the Kitwancool. B.C. Provincial Museum, Victoria 1959

Efrat, Barbara S. and W.J. Langlois (Hg.): nu·tka· – The History and Survival of Nootkan Culture. Provincial Archives of B.C., Victoria 1978

Fisher, Robin: Contact and Conflict. Indian-European Relations in British Columbia, 1774–1890. University of B.C. Press, Vancouver 1977

Gerber, Peter R. (Hg.): Vom Recht, Indianer zu sein. Menschenrechte und Landrechte der Indianer beider Amerika. Ethnologische Schriften Zürich Nr. 4, 1986

Gerber, Peter R. and Georges Ammann: Die Nordwestküsten-Indianer. Zur Kultur, Geschichte und Gegenwartssituation. Materialien und Vorschläge für den Unterricht. Pestalozzianum Zürich & Völkerkundemuseum der Universität Zürich, 1988 (im Druck)

Haberland, Wolfgang: Donnervogel und Raubwal. Die indianische Kunst der Nordwestküste Nordamerikas. Museum für Völkerkunde, Hamburg 1979

Hall, Edwin S., Jr., Margaret B. Blackmann and Vincent Rickard: Northwest Coast Indian Graphics. An Introduction to Silk Screen Prints. Douglas & McIntyre, Vancouver 1981

Halpin, Marjorie M.: Totem Poles. An Illustrated Guide. University of B.C. Press, Vancouver 1981

Harris, Chief Kenneth B.: Visitors Who Never Left. The Origin of the People of Damelahamid. (With F.M.P. Robinson), University of B.C. Press, Vancouver 1974

Hawthorn, Audrey: Kwakiutl Art. Douglas & McIntyre, Vancouver 1979

Hill, Beth and Ray Hill: Indian Petroglyphs of the Pacific and Northwest. Hancock House. Saanichton, B.C. 1974

Holm, Bill: Northwest Coast Indian Art. An Analysis of Form. University of Washington Press, Seattle 1965

Holm, Bill: The Box of Daylight. Northwest Coast Indian Art. Douglas & McIntyre, Vancouver 1983; University of Washington Press, Seattle 1983

Holm, Bill: Smoky-Top. The Art and Times of Willie Seaweed. Douglas & McIntyre, Vancouver 1983

Holm, Bill and Bill Reid: Indian Art of the Northwest Coast. University of Washington Press, Seattle 1975

Jorgensen, Joseph G.: Western Indians. Comparative Environments, Languages, and Cultures of 172 Western American Indian Tribes. Freeman, San Francisco 1980

Kenyon, Susan M.: The Kyuquot Way: A Study of a West Coast (Nootkan) Community. National Museum of Man, Ottawa 1980

Kirk, Ruth: Hunters of the Whale. An Adventure in Northwest Coast Archaeology. (With Richard D. Daugherty), Morrow, New York 1974

Laguna, Frederica de: Under Mount Saint Elias: The History and Culture of the Yakutat Tlingit. Smithsonian Institution Press, Washington, D.C. 1972

MacDonald, George F.: Ninstints. Haida World Heritage Site. University of B.C. Press, Vancouver 1983

MacDonald, George F.: Totem Poles and Monuments of Gitwangak Village. Parks Canada, Ottawa 1984

Macnair, Peter L., Alan L. Hoover and Kevin Neary: The Legacy. Continuing Traditions of Canadian Northwest Coast Indian Art. B.C. Provincial Museum, Victoria 1980

Miller, Jay and Carol M. Eastman (Hg.): The Tsimshian and Their Neighbors of the North Pacific Coast. University of Washington Press, Seattle 1984

People of K'san: Gathering What the Great Nature Provided. Food Traditions of the Gitskan. Douglas & McIntyre, Vancouver 1980

Samuel, Cheryl: The Chilkat Dancing Blanket. Pacific Search Press, Seattle 1982; University of Oklahoma, Norman 1989

Seguin, Margaret (Hg.): The Tsimshian. Images of the Past: Views for the Present. University of B.C. Press, Vancouver 1984

Stearns, Mary Lee: Haida Culture in Custody. The Masset Band. University of Washington Press, Seattle 1981

Stewart, Hilary: Indian Fishing. Early Methods on the Northwest Coast. Douglas & McIntyre, Vancouver 1977; University of Washington Press, Seattle 1977

Stewart, Hilary: Cedar. Tree of Life to the Northwest Coast Indians. Douglas & McIntyre, Vancouver 1984; University of Washington Press, Seattle 1984

Vaughan, Thomas and Bill Holm: Soft Gold. The Fur Trade and Cultural Exchange on the Northwest Coast of America. Oregon Historical Society, Portland 1989

INDEX

231

ACKNOWLEDGMENTS

The authors thank the following persons and institutions for their valuable help and support with this project:

Roxana J. Adams, Totem Heritage Center & Tongass Historical Museum, Ketchikan
Greig W. Arnold, Makah Cultural Center, Neah Bay, Wash.
Bill Assa, Kwakiutl Museum, Quathiaski Cove, B.C.
Harris L. and Solomon D. Atkinson, Metlakatla
David and Elizabeth Boxley, Metlakatla
Holly Churchill-Burns, Ketchikan
Jeanne Carter, Vancouver Indian Centre Society
Annette McFadyen Clark, National Museum of Man, Ottawa
Peter L. Corey, Sheldon Jackson Museum, Sitka
Marcelle Dumoulin, Canadian Embassy, Bern
Christian F. Feest, Museum für Völkerkunde, Vienna
Trisha Gessler, Queen Charlotte I. Museum, Skidegate
Conrad E.W. Graham, McCord Museum, Montreal
Howard Green, Native Education Centre, Vancouver
Margaret Gross, Indian Cultural Center, Sitka
Ellen Hays, Indian Cultural Center, Sitka
Carl and Lee Heinmiller, Chilkat-Dancers, Haines
Karl H. Henking, VM, Zürich
Richard Hunt, Victoria
Tony Hunt, Victoria
Estelle Inman, Kwakiutl Museum, Quathiaski Cove, B.C.
Nathan P. Jackson, Ketchikan
Harold Jacobs, Indian Cultural Center, Sitka
Alan Jay, Indian and Northern Affairs Canada, Vancouver
David R. Johnson, Metlakatla
Elizabeth L. Johnson, Museum of Anthropology, Vancouver
Harry and Peter Johnson, Chilkat-Dancers, Haines
Art Jones, Pacheenaht First Nation, Port Renfrew, B.C.
Charles King, Jr., Klukwan, Alaska
Sue Kinnear, Sitka National Historical Park , Sitka
James H. Kirk, American Embassy, Bern
Suellen Liljeblad, Tongass Historical Museum, Ketchikan
Peter L. Macnair, B.C. Provincial Museum, Victoria
Louis Minard, Indian Cultural Center, Sitka
Richard Parcival, Union of B.C. Indian Chiefs, Vancouver
Tim Paul, Victoria
Reggie B. Peterson, Indian Cultural Center, Sitka
Audrey Shane, Museum of Anthropology, Vancouver
Hilary Stewart, Vancouver
Saul Terry, Union of B.C. Indian Chiefs, Vancouver
Edward K. Thomas, Tlingit & Haida Central Council, Juneau
Lynn A. Wallen, Alaska State Museum, Juneau
Ed and Patricia Warren, Kluckwan, Alaska
Pat Watson, Wrangell Museum, Wrangell
Gloria Webster, U.Bär Verlag, Zürich
Ronald D. Williams, Alaska Native Brotherhood, Juneau

Eva and Maximillien Bruggman give special thanks for hospitality and contributions to the following:

Pat Alfred, Nimkish First Nation, Alert Bay, B.C.

Pat Alfred, Nimkish First Nation, Alert Bay, B.C.
Ruth and Willi Blaser, North-Vancouver
Monique and Michel Commend, Montreal
Freda Diesing, Terrace, B.C.
Celine and Pierre Forand, Sandspit, B.C.
Stan Greene, Chilliwack, B.C.
François A. Montandon, Calgary, Alberta
Ken Mowatt, Hazelton
Peter Müller, Montreal
Peter Nebel, VM, Zürich
Susan A. Point, Vancouver
John Reichen and Family, Portland, Oregon
Hanne and Victor Schott, Los Angeles, California
Roy H. Vickers, Tofino, B.C.

Peter R. Gerber is especially grateful to:

Andrea Laforet, National Museum of Man, Ottawa
James V. Leslie, Alert Bay
John F. Leslie, Indian and Northern Affairs Canada, Ottawa
Brenda McGregor, Assembly of First Nations, Ottawa
Malcolm McSporran, Quilicum-Restaurant, Vancouver
Louise Mandell, Union of B.C. Indian Chiefs, Vancouver
Linna and Ludger Müller-Wille, Montreal
Helen Ryan, Indian and Northern Affairs Canada, Ottawa
Beverly Sommer, Vancouver Museum
Norman K. Zlotkin, University of Saskatchewan, Saskatoon
. . . and above all to:
Elisabeth Biasio, VM, Zürich
Ruth and Mark Phillips, Carleton University, Ottawa
Peter Reese, Vancouver

Abbreviations

ASM	Alaska State Museum, Juneau
GA	Glenbow Archives, Calgary
ICC	Southeast Alaska Indian Cultural Center, Sitka
MM	McCord Museum, McGill University, Montreal
MOA	Museum of Anthropology, University of British Columbia, Vancouver
NMM	National Museum of Man, Ottawa
PM	British Columbia Provincial Museum, Victoria
ROM	Royal Ontario Museum, Toronto
SJM	Sheldon Jackson Museum, Sitka
SNHP	Sitka National Historical Park, Sitka
VM	Völkerkundemuseum der Universität Zürich